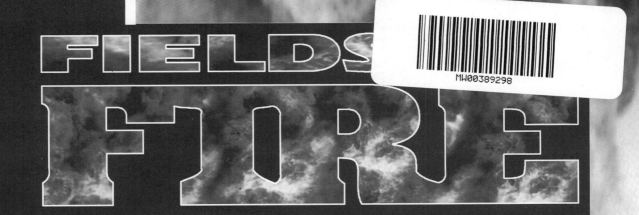

FIELDS OF FIRE

FASA CORPORATION

CONTENTS

FIELDS OF FIRE

Design and Writing
Tom Dowd

Development
Tom Dowd

Editorial Staff
Editorial Director
Donna Ippolito
Managing Editor
Sharon Turner Mulvihill
Associate Editors
Diane Piron-Gelman
Rob Cruz

Production Staff
Art Director
Jim Nelson
Project Manager
Mark Ernst
Cover Art
Louis Royo
Cover Design
Mark Ernst
Illustrations
Earl Geier
Mike Jackson
Rick Harris
Layout
Mark Ernst
Keyline and Paste up
Ernesto Hernandez

Published by FASA Corporation, 1100 W. Cermak Rd., Ste. B305
Chicago, Il 60608

FASA Corporation can be reached on the GEnie computer network (E. Mail—
FASA.SUPPORT) on SCORPIA'S Roundtable (page 805) and on America
OnLine (E. Mail— FASATom (Shadowrun), FASALou (Earthdawn), FASABryan
(BattleTech) or FASAMike (General Harassment)) in the Online Gaming area
(Keyword "Gaming"). Via InterNet use <AOL Account Name>@AOL>COM, but
please, no list or server subscriptions. Thanks!

INTRODUCTION

Fields of Fire is a sourcebook for mercenary characters in the **Shadowrun** universe. Because the **Shadowrun** game is not just about mercs or purely mercenary operations, this sourcebook focuses on how merc characters think and behave in relation to the usual **Shadowrun** storyline. This sourcebook is about attitude and purpose.

The **Field Pack** section is devoted to weapons and equipment available mainly to mercenaries, but also to the most savvy street samurai. The **Rules** section in the back of this book expands and clarifies certain existing combat rules and offers new optional rules.

Enjoy!

WELCOME TO...

SHADOWLAND

"I have taken all knowledge to be my province."
— Francis Bacon, 1592

CATEGORY

GO TO:

Message Base/Mail System — OK

Special Category/Topics (SIGS) — OK

Library Archive — OK

Information Base — SPECIAL FEATURES (Limited Duration Posting) — OK

Paranormal Animals of Europe (Don't say we didn't warn ya. . .) — OK

Corporate Shadowfiles (Corp Dirt! Dig In!) — OK

Denver Compilation (Treaty City Stuff!) — NOT AVAILABLE

Shadowtech Compilation (Weird Science 101) — OK

Fields of Fire (Mercs and Guns!!) — OK

Tír na nÓg (Available!) — OK

&&^BMSJAIDMJIO&(#@*Q& ??? — OK

Real Life Compilation (Real Cool!) — OK

Lone Star Security Uncovered!!! (Soon!) — NOT AVAILABLE

Germany (We got it!) — OK

Tir Tairngire (Those Wacky Elves. . .™) — OK

FIELDS OF FIRE

Introduction — OK

Fields of Fire (Merc Manual) — OK

Field Pack (Weapons and Gear) — OK

DOWNLOAD ALL? OK

NOTE FROM CONTROL—Anyone with any knowledge regarding sabotage to this system should contact me ASAP. Censorship will not be tolerated!

FIELDS OF FIRE

The text of this file is abridged and revised from the volume of the same name, written by Juan Samuel Pererya and published by World Independent Press, Miami, FL, 2048 (Second Edition).

MERCENARY OPERATIONS

I am a mercenary.

>>>>>(As a point of interest, Juan Samuel Pererya posts in these parts under the handle Matador. If I'm not mistaken, he's posting these days from a Peruvian hospital (or some similar place). A few of his postings appear in the Field Pack section of this upload—which, oddly enough, seems to have been compiled backwards. The Field Pack equipment section is an older posting; you can tell by the dates. Who knows why it ended up second in the file sequence? I don't know if Matador will post comments on his own work, but it'll be more interesting if he does.)<<<<<
—Colonel Cobra (12:19:28/01-02-55)

>>>>>(By the way, since this is a public posting (to be echoed after the usual annotation) I expect a lot of non-mercs to be perusing these pages. A non-merc myself, I found the contents interesting stuff. I've read through it once, and log back in every so often to annotate it myself where necessary.

I think this material is of value to everyone, not just mercs. Pererya says a lot in here about how we should act and behave toward each other (shadowrunners take note!), so pay attention. Professionalism shouldn't be limited to self-proclaimed professionals. It's a code we should all follow. Lord knows I'd feel safer walking the shadow-streets if we did.)<<<<<
—Hatchetman (03:19:50/01-04-54)

One of the dictionaries on my computer defines the term mercenary in two ways: a) One who works or acts merely for money or other reward, or b) A professional soldier serving in a foreign army solely for pay.

I cannot dispute the letter of what each says.

I once asked a young relative of mine (who believed I worked in the international import/export business, an old and respected cover) what he thought the term "mercenary" meant. He told me mercenaries were people who went someplace else and killed people for money.

I cannot honestly dispute his definition.

>>>>>(Yeah, no drek you can't. Wonder why?)<<<<<
—Smiley (21:17:17/01-04-55)

>>>>>(Shut up and read, sludge brain.)<<<<<
—Weasel (03:29:16/01-06-55)

I can, however, explain what the term mercenary means to me. This may take some time, so bear with me.

WHAT IS A MERCENARY?

I am a soldier, pure and simple. I am trained in the ways of modern warfare and schooled in the theories of the ancients. I do what people who consider themselves humane believe is unnecessary in our modern world.

I use force to accomplish an end.

It's a simple, age-old problem. You want something done. Someone or something stands in your way. But what you want done is important. It cannot be left undone. What do you do? What alternatives do you have? What price will you pay to achieve your goal?

>>>>>(He makes a valid point, one a lot of people tend to forget. What happens when negotiating doesn't work? We've become so afraid of war, or, more precisely, its price in blood, that we knee jerk toward negotiation and compromise. Unfortunately, talking sometimes just doesn't work, especially when someone wants something very badly.

There's a remake of some old pop tune making the rounds these days, and one of its lyrics goes something like this: "I don't know no military solution that didn't end up as something worse." Sorry, chummer, whoever you were—like it or not, I can think of plenty that did what they were supposed to do.)<<<<<
—Conjoiner (20:51:54/01-03-55)

>>>>>(Yeah, but isn't it a good thing that we so quickly reject a military solution? Isn't prudence sometimes better? Many military solutions *have* failed, and with disastrous results, because the people in charge thought they understood what was going on and only succeeded in making things worse. Maybe thinking twice and trying everything else three times isn't such a bad thing.)<<<<<
—Findler-man (03:28:16/01-05-55)

Some people would have you believe that only two alternatives exist: peace and war. Though we can learn much from the practice of Taoism and the wisdom of the ancients, things are not always as simple as wet or dry, white or black, soft or hard, peace or war. Sometimes you have both.

That's where I come in.

A mercenary's job involves much more than simply waging war on someone else's payroll. War is pain and death and misery. War is not something humans desire. It is, however, something we must accept when there are no alternatives. If we believe strongly that something must be done, we may have to fight for it. By the same token, if we do not believe strongly, we should not fight.

But we must make that decision before we begin. Once we begin, we can't turn back.

Force must be applied with intelligence. Anyone can fire a submachine gun into a crowd. Anyone can push a button and launch a missile that slaughters a hundred children. Anyone can kill. It's easy.

A mercenary knows how to kill. He also knows when not to kill. He knows that sometimes, simply being strong is enough. He knows that the threat of violence can bring about peace—time and again, history has proved this truth. He knows that one man or group of men in the right place at the right time can save hundreds from death.

He also knows that sometimes, talking isn't enough. And he stands ready for that moment.

>>>>>(Yeah, he loves that moment. He sits in the dark, quivering, waiting for that moment.)<<<<<
—Smiley (21:19:08/01-04-55)

>>>>>(Geez, what's with you?)<<<<<
—Weasel (03:31:54/01-06-55)

BEING A MERCENARY

Not everyone is cut out to be a mercenary.

It takes a certain kind of individual to be a mercenary. A mercenary understands herself, her abilities, and her limitations. She knows her role in the world, what she is expected to do, and what lies outside her responsibility. She can dream, but holds no illusions about reality. Most of all, she understands the intelligent application of force. As dangerous and horrific as it can be, she understands it as a valuable and effective tool.

She understands people. She knows how their minds work, how they think when they are calm, how they react when they are afraid. She understands what people want, from basic sustenance to decadent luxury, and she knows the lengths to which people will go to get what they want. She knows how to reason with others, how to explain her own and her opponent's position, how to listen and make others listen.

The mercenary is always prepared. She knows her equipment and her weapons. She knows what she needs and where to get it. She knows the requirements of her assignment and the equipment needed to get the job done.

>>>>>(I'll attest to that! We've stopped getting our combat gear through our local fixer, and now use one of our teammate's old merc contacts, his dealer. Takes longer, and sometimes pickups get a little complicated, but the quality of the stuff that shows up is first-rate.)<<<<<
—Wenton Warrior (08:27:40/01-06-55)

Above everything else, the mercenary knows her job. She's analyzed it, dissected it, and put it back together in every possible combination. She knows what's supposed to happen and what might happen, and she's prepared for those times when things don't go as expected.

She is a professional.

>>>>>(Professional what? (yuck hyuck))<<<<<
—Smiley (21:23:54/01-04-55)

>>>>>(Chummer, if you hadn't logged on two days ago I'd trace and burn your butt from here to Kansas City.)<<<<<
—Weasel (03:35:35/01-06-55)

BASIC OPERATIONS

Many people mistakenly believe that because a mercenary works freelance, he does not live by any rules. In fact, mercenaries are professionals, and like all professionals, live by a certain set of rules. A mercenary must value and practice personal discipline, interpersonal skills, preparedness, and controlled orientation and exposure. I touched on these requirements in a general way already, but because these issues lie at the heart of being a mercenary, this next section expounds on each requirement in detail.

These abilities are the basics, the things you must know, digest, and make your own before you begin your career as a mercenary. Even seasoned professionals need to review these basics from time to time, because the years of work tend to make you forget. Never forget.

PERSONAL DISCIPLINE

I live by a code. Most mercenaries do. A merc without a personal code is nothing more than a sociopath with no concern beyond himself. Mercenaries are not madmen.

>>>>>(Some might argue that point, but this is not the forum in which to contest it. Personally, I think there's a little something loose in the head of anyone who chooses the life of a merc—or one in the shadows, for that matter.)<<<<<
—Normal PEE (21:39:02/01-05-55)

The process of discovering your code, what you will and will not allow yourself to do, takes a lifetime's worth of learning. It never ends, for any of us.

Before you choose the mercenary's life, you must determine your own code. Find out where you believe the lines are drawn. This knowledge is very important.

>>>>>(It is not just important. It's mandatory. If you don't establish a code for your life, you'll soon find yourself flopping compulsively from cause to cause, caring less and less about human life. God, is it important. Find your code. Live by it.)<<<<<
—Winter Rat (23:19:20/01-06-55)

I became comfortable with my code many years ago, but I know that I am an exception to the rule. I became a mercenary for my own reasons. Though my history shares much with that of other mercenaries, certain, singular things in my heart and mind define me. They color everything that happens to me and shape the way I see the world. Every person possesses individual, unusual perspectives and thoughts that shape his or her world view. Find yours and learn what they mean as quickly as you can.

Because my experience may help others formulate their own codes, or at least give them something to think about, I'm writing down the broadest precepts of my personal code. I keep the specifics nailed down in my head, but those won't matter to anyone except me.

>>>>>(If Matador's specifics do matter to you, here's a tidbit—Matador is Mexican. Note that I said Mexican, not Aztlaner. That distinction is important.)<<<<<
—Night Hunter (02:19:14/01-08-55)

•*I take only jobs I believe in.* Before I contract for a job, I learn all I can about the work and the situation, and not just from the client. I do my own research and learn as much of the truth as possible. Sometimes, especially with secret operations, I can't learn much. In those situations I trust my fixer. He and I have a long-established relationship; he knows me and knows the kind of jobs I won't do.

>>>>>(Basically, learn when to say NO! It's easy, really, and ultimately it earns you a lot of respect. Don't get caught on some testosterone wave and take a job because your machismo demands it. If your guts don't like it, turn it down.)<<<<<
—Uncle Paul (11:08:47/01-06-55)

•*I do not take jobs offered solely because of my ability to kill.* I am not a professional killer. Though killing is often part of my profession, I cannot be hired exclusively to kill. I admit that his part of my code may wander into a gray area, because I have done wet work in the past and will probably do it again. (Wet work, for those who don't know, is assassination for hire.) But I am not a professional assassin. The wet work I've performed has always been one element of a larger operation, admittedly sometimes the principal objective of that operation. The difference between me and a professional assassin lies in the first part of my code. I take only jobs I believe in. If performing a job I believe in means people must die, I accept this. I live with it.

>>>>>(Notice the important subtext running through much of this abstract: Kill only when necessary. I prefer to forget the number of runs I've been on that were filled with gratuitous killing. I don't work with jokers like that twice. Few people do, because soon they'll have so many corps and cops after them that no one will want to hire them. Don't kill unless you have to. Non-lethal tactics work just as well as lethal ones most times, and don't create the same kind of enemies.)<<<<<
—Hatchetman (04:10:18/01-08-55)

•*I am not judge, jury, and executioner.* I am not the law. The society and civilization we live in accepts some things and reviles others. I make my judgment calls based on the precepts of that society. Are the objectives of my job acceptable or even beneficial to society as a whole? Am I helping to advance some worthy cause? If not, I don't take the job, or I refuse to fulfill the objective. I live and work by my conscience and my code.

•*I walk away if things change.* Sometimes, the truth is different from the inside. Once an operation begins, certain things become evident that could not be seen before. If this new truth changes the way I view an operation so that I would not have taken the operation if I had known those truths going in, I will walk away from that operation. I have walked away, and it has cost me money, prestige, work, and friendships. I make sure my employer understands this part of my code before I begin the operation. My attitude has affected the kind of jobs I get and given me a certain reputation. I like that.

•*I value all human life.* I value both friend and foe. I will not betray my friends or my allies for the "cause." Yes, I sometimes need to make hard decisions, but I will not work with the knowledge that those decisions must be made as part of the operation.

I especially value the life of my opposition. You'll note that I don't say "enemy." I do not assume my opponent is my enemy. My opponents believe, perhaps as strongly as I do, that *they* are doing something important. They have values, a code perhaps, and most important, they also have lives. I have no inherent right to take that life. Don't misunderstand me: I fully understand that killing may be required, but I will not kill needlessly. Yes, I consider injury a viable alternative to death. I would gladly injure someone, even permanently disable them, to remove that person as a threat rather than kill them. Killing may not be necessary, but it does come with the territory.

Have I ever violated my code? Yes. It troubled me deeply every time. But I'm glad it disturbs me to do so. That's how I know I'm human.

>>>>>(I know Matador, and I envy him his code. Many people in our line of work wrestle with their consciences almost daily, and that constant struggle makes me wonder why some people become mercenaries. For the glory? There isn't much. For the thrill? Too many get involved this way. For the money? Become an accountant. The corps always need more accountants.

Personally, the Euro-Wars left me without a place in society. Combat affected me so deeply that the scars from what I'd experienced began killing me once the war stopped. The only way I could keep my mind intact was to tear those wounds open each time they started to heal. Has it helped? Am I sane because of it? I don't know.)<<<<<
—Colonel Cobra (03:20:18/01-05-55)

INTERPERSONAL SKILLS

Don't deceive yourself. You can't be a successful mercenary by "letting your gun speak for you." That cliché will get you killed. You are a professional, and you must always behave like one.

As a professional soldier you must know how to communicate, how to send and receive messages. Communication takes many forms, and written and oral language represents only a minor area of true communication. Simply by stating "I am a mercenary," you are sending a message. The base level of that particular message, however, has little or nothing to do with *you*. What that message communicates relies almost completely on the receiving person's perception of a mercenary's role. If they believe that mercenaries are soulless killers, then they will deal with you on that basis. If they believe that a mercenary is a professional who knows his job and is prepared to do it, then your statement communicates that notion to them. Initially, it does not matter what message you intend to send. What they believe defines their interpretation of the message they receive.

If they perceive something different from what you intend, you must convince them otherwise.

>>>>>(Many people live in a vacuum of understanding. They view the world through their own frame of reference, refusing to accept what other people hear or see as valid. They don't realize that much of what each of us knows (or believes we know) clouds our perceptions. Think about the many tragedies that could have been avoided if people paid attention to the messages they were sending and how others perceived those messages.)<<<<<
—Doc Tanner (20:14:27/01-09-55)

You can only convince people of what you really represent through skilled communication. You tell everyone you meet who and what you are in four ways: the ways you speak, write, act, and look.

Don't dismiss this as nonessential. I cannot exaggerate the importance of communication skills to a professional soldier. You must constantly be aware of how others perceive you, because their perceptions control their behavior toward you. What you actually intend means nothing in the face of what they believe of you.

How to Speak

Speak well, speak clearly. Make sure they understand you. When on duty, make every verbal communication with your superiors a formal communication. This holds true whether your superiors are your friends or you think they are dog scum. You are a professional.

Learn to speak the local language from a native. If you learn it from a chip or rely on a linguasoft, the natives will get the message that you don't care enough to learn the language properly. If you speak the local language unassisted by technology, you send the message that you are willing to spend the necessary time to learn about the local culture. You are willing to spend the time to learn how to speak to them. That's a powerful message.

Learn *how* the locals speak. Do they speak loudly? Softly? Using direct eye contact? Emulate the locals rather than mimicking them, and don't attempt to do it perfectly. You probably can't, and it's better to acknowledge the fact that you are an outsider who respects their culture than to embarrass yourself and them by performing badly. If you mess up, you appear to mock their traditions.

>>>>>(Day-to-day corporate life teaches the same lesson with regard to the Japanese megacorps. How long has the West maintained corporate relations with the Japanese? A century? How many billions of nuyen have the corps spent on research, analysis, and training? Can a *gaijin* bow correctly yet? Nope, yet they keep right on trying.)<<<<<
 —Mr. Yota-san (20:19:27/01-10-55)

Do not speak to the locals as if they are subordinates. These people live where you work. You are their guest, even if you work for their government.

Your profession means that people will listen very carefully to what you say to find the message they expect. Because you are a mercenary, others will believe you deceptive, hiding things behind doublespeak. Be clear. Be concise. Allow no room for doubt or misunderstanding.

How to Write

Write clearly and concisely. Make sure they understand you. To tell the truth, I do little writing in the field. Between jobs, however, I can easily fill my time with after-action reports, supply and inventory requests, mission-planning documents, and so on. And though I may not actually write the first draft (I prefer speech-recognition dictation into my pocket secretary) I always proof the final document to make sure that it is complete and looks professional, and that it doesn't sound like I wrote it off-

the-cuff. Even the most well-structured, formal speech reads poorly when written unless you edit it.

Learn to write the local language. In this case, chip-based literacy is usually good enough because written language tends to be more formal. Languages based on pictographic character sets constitute an exception to this rule. Because even the most advanced linguasoft often provides somewhat rough pictograph depiction, have a trustworthy native proficient in the written language check the lettering. Everyone who reads your communications will attempt to read between the lines, and will look long and hard to find whatever they think you are not telling them. Your only useful response is to leave nothing to interpretation. Be clear. Be concise.

Avoid written communication whenever possible. Even my mind boggles at the number of times I've heard that operational security was compromised because someone wrote down sensitive information. If you must keep notes or, God forbid, a diary (I can think of few actions more idiotic for a merc), write in a personal symbolic code. Don't use a cipher—ciphers can be easily broken. A code in which a single symbol sub-references an entire concept and augments the following symbols is much harder to break. Your opponent will need you to translate such a code—and don't be naive; they'll make you do it.

How to Act

The way you act may be your most important method of communication. I have known many talented men and women who think that holding a position of power or carrying a gun gives them the right to act like children. In fact, just the opposite is true.

>>>>>(Working the streets proves the ugly truth of what Matador says here. I've been at countless meets where the participants were copping the juvenile "wiz 'tude" one-upmanship program. If I have to watch one more street sam clean his blades during a negotiation, I'll vomit. What's the point, other than pure narcissism? (And I apologize to all you street sams who will have to look that word up.))<<<<<
 —Hatchetman (04:24:28/01-06-55)

>>>>>(Hey Hatchet, I thought you were a street sam?)<<<<<
 —Global Warmer (23:29:18/01-06-55)

>>>>>(I am. Trust me—I know all about them.)<<<<<
 —Hatchetman (20:10:16/01-08-55)

The cliché is old but true: with power comes responsibility. I've said it at least a dozen times already: you are a professional. You must act like a professional at all times. How you act reflects on you, your allies, and others in your profession.

Your actions send the most powerful messages about who and what you are. Even a person who believes you a soulless killer may change her mind over time when presented with behavior that refutes that belief.

I cannot create a comprehensive list of acceptable and unacceptable actions, but I can offer some guidelines based on my own experience. Fully exploring each of the following guidelines could require an entire book per guideline, but until I write those books, I can only hope that the short explanations and examples will spark a little understanding.

•*Avoid non-professional relationships while on the job.* This short sentence covers a great many things. Don't become friends with your client—keep that relationship clearly defined. Develop a trusting, familiar, business relationship with your team members or allies, but don't befriend them. (Save that for downtime. You can act buddy-buddy, but do not develop an emotional attachment during the operation. What bonds people under stress is different from what bonds people during the calm. I find that friendships developed during the calm are far stronger.) Avoid sexual relationships of any kind; they only increase your vulnerability to blackmail or manipulation. Sexual relationships can also lead to emotional bonds that could jeopardize the operation.

>>>>>(I don't know about this one. Ya see, Matador has spent a lot of time isolating himself from emotional associations that could harm him. Despite this, he has an amazing ability to sympathize and empathize with all types of people. I've seen it happen. What he does, though, is abstracts it. He sympathizes with the *situation*. He empathizes with the *plight*. He sees the problem as it affects many people, not just one person. One person could hurt him.)<<<<<
—Winter Rat (19:02:17/01-09-55)

•*Play it straight.* Because you are ultimately only a hired hand, your best option is to shoot straight. For as long as the operation lasts, your only loyalty is to your client. This stays true unless you learn something you didn't know when you began the operation that violates your personal code. Even in that situation, play it straight. Protect yourself, but lay your cards on the table.

>>>>>(Are you fraggers paying attention? THIS IS IMPORTANT ON THE STREETS. You know the saying, "It ain't a shadowrun unless your Johnson has screwed you twice?" You know why that's true? 'Cause the Johnsons think shadowrunners are scum, and rightly so. Merc employers don't have this attitude, and neither do people who hire other kinds of freelancers. Why does this attitude stick to shadowrunners? 'Cause these people are fools! They heap crap on the Johnson. They act barely professional. They don't make plans, or even think things through. They create nearly as much trouble on the run as the run was supposed to solve, and they have no respect for each other or the people paying them. They aren't professionals in any sense of the word. They're thugs.)<<<<<
—Hatchetman (20:17:18/01-08-55)

>>>>>(Gee, Hatchet, having a quality control problem?)<<<<<
—`Shroom (09:20:19/01-10-55)

>>>>>(Fraggin' right I am, and I'm full-throttle tired of it. I kicked the drek out of a decker two days ago because he skimmed a corporate datastore we were explicitly told

not to skim. What's his excuse? "They're a corp; who's gonna know?" How about me? How about him? How about our employer, since they know exactly when we were in there? How about the corp we ran against that just might be willing to absorb the damage? If the decker skimmed something damn valuable and the corp finds out, who'll be twisting in the wind then?)<<<<<
—Hatchetman (18:28:20/01-11-55)

>>>>>(Careful, Hatchetman. We know you're blowing off steam, but you don't want to be slammin' deckers 'round these parts.)<<<<<
—Findler-man (19:19:18/01-12-55)

•*Play it smart.* Know when to say no. Don't allow yourself to be drawn into positions detrimental to your health or security just because it seems to be part of the game. Don't allow yourself to be goaded into acting stupidly. Your opposition (and perhaps someone on your own side) is waiting for you to make a mistake. Stay in control. Don't allow yourself to be manipulated or jerked around.

•*Be a professional.* Everything I talk about in this book, *everything*, should become an integral, reflexive part of your life. None of the advice written here can be ignored even for a moment. Your life may depend on it. More than once I've been in a bad situation, on the losing side, but I walked away in one piece because I maintained my professionalism. People respect that, even if they don't respect what you do. I'll discuss another big part of this particular point later on: odds are, you'll be facing other professionals, other mercs. Respect runs both ways.

>>>>>(True, true, especially in the merc's field of operations. I've watched a merc field commander calmly eating lunch with his captured merc adversary with a complete lack of special security precautions or even a hint of worry, simply because they're both merc. Boggled my mind at first, but then I realized it's all part of this code thing. Warfare is hell, and they're the ones who do it for the ones who won't. All this code stuff is just one way of keeping themselves sane.)<<<<<
—Merc-On-Training Wheels (20:42:59/01-09-55)

How to Dress

Don't stop reading now. You may think that discussing a merc's outfit sounds pretty dumb, but how you dress sends a specific message. People base their responses to you on what they think they know (preconceptions) and what they experience (perceptions). If I see a merc on dress duty looking rumpled, I question his commitment. If I see an off-duty merc out carousing and looking like gutter filth, I question his discretion. If I see a merc walk into the local watering-hole-cum-opposition-hangout in full-dress khakis, I question his sanity.

>>>>>(Oh, yeah. Remember that street sam I mentioned before who was cleaning his blades while we negotiated with a Johnson? Did I mention he had the top of his head shaved, and what little hair remained was down to his shoulder blades and bone white? Did I also mention that he had tattooed on his bald head the words BITE MY SNAKE? During the whole meeting, I could see the Johnson looking this guy over and wondering just what kind of people he was hiring.)<<<<<
—Hatchetman (20:29:09/01-08-55)

>>>>>(Does he actually have a snake?)<<<<<
—`Shroom (09:25:09/01-10-55)

>>>>>(Yeah, a red-and-brown anaconda named Freddi.)<<<<<
—Hatchetman (18:34:58/01-11-55)

In general, ask yourself how another person would react listening to you, conversing with you, or just watching you. Does everything about you send the message that you are smart, alert, serious, skilled, perhaps dangerous, and definitely a professional? When you send that message, you'll be surprised by how much easier your job gets.

PREPAREDNESS

Never take a job blind. Before you agree to the terms of a contract, do your own research, learn everything you can. Check with your contacts. Listen to the people you trust. Scan the media, but pay attention to who is saying what. Everyone, *everyone*, speaks from a bias or private agenda of some sort. If you recognize that bias or agenda, you can use it to your advantage.

>>>>>(Yeah—if the government-run radio station *isn't* shouting the news about how well its troops are doing in the mountains hunting down the rebels. . .)<<<<<
—Media Watcher II (21:58:09/01-11-55)

Take nothing for granted. As part of the contract, your client may offer to provide you with everything you need. Thank him graciously, but let him know in the most professional way possible that you prefer to make all arrangements yourself. If he is a professional, he'll understand.

Learn everything you can about your target zone, your area of operations. Use maps, pictures, trideo, first-hand accounts, everything available. Absorb it, file it, database it: you'll need it. Research other operations performed in the area. Why did they succeed or fail? What were their strengths and weaknesses?

>>>>>(Personally, I know I'm in trouble when the team I'm leading has a planning meeting and the response to my suggestion that we track down and debrief other runners who've pulled a run against our target is a table full of vapid stares. Then some wit says: "We can do that?")<<<<<

—Hatchetman (04:20:18/01-12-55)

Consider the "why" as well as the "where." *Never* enter a situation ignorant of local politics. That's the fastest way to get yourself dead. Why is your employer mounting this operation? What short- and long-term results does he expect? Who profits from a successful operation? Who gets hurt? Analyze all the players involved, and learn their strengths and weaknesses.

Study a breakdown of your timetable. You can often determine important information from the time that things occur. For example, does your employer expect you to wrap up the operation before spring? Why? Keep

a careful eye on weather and climate projections. It's an amateur's mistake to be caught flat-footed by the weather, but it's amazingly easy to overlook that factor.

Finally, plan every step of the operation in detail. Consider what you need in terms of manpower, equipment, and transportation. Arrange as many of these elements as possible yourself. Rely on your own contacts and resources in order to reduce the chance of "unexpected exposure." Again, if your client is a professional, he'll understand your methods. If forced to work with local resources, inspect those resources personally as early in the operation as possible. Don't trust your life to other people's skill with machinery or inventory. Trust only your own abilities.

Much of this advice assumes that you are in a position of authority. Even if you are not, learn these lessons well. If you take this advice to heart, you can more easily educate yourself about the wasp's nest you may land in. Preparation is the best defense against any situation.

ORIENTATION AND EXPOSURE

Control your orientation and exposure by making your own travel arrangements. Simple, but important. Naturally, you need to inform your client of when and where you will meet, but you need to establish certain responsibilities early in the relationship. The employer hires you to perform a specific function; in order to effectively perform all roles appropriate to that function, you must control your own security as much as possible. Because self-sufficiency is part of a merc's professionalism, your client should understand. Thank him graciously and use your own travel agent.

Your security work really begins when you reach your area of operations. Be aware of everything around you, all the time. Regardless of your location or your assignment, you were hired to do something that poses a threat to someone. Smart opponents will try to derail your operation before it begins. In the field you are always vulnerable, and you must devote constant effort to minimizing your exposure.

>>>>>(And you know, the corps never have their ears to the ground listening for a buncha steel-toed shadowrunners tromping through the urban jungle, conducting legwork like they were on safari.)<<<<<
—Jet Jaguar (20:51:38/01-12-55)

>>>>>(Geez, Jet, you sitting on the other end of the stick that's up Hatchetman's butt?)<<<<<
—Found Finster! (13:28:29/01-13-55)

In merc terms, exposure refers to your vulnerability, both personally and in terms of the operation. Security is paramount. You must keep your operation secure at all times, beginning long before you reach the operational zone.

Never advertise your presence. When you reconnoiter your operational area to gather information, never reveal your identity or purpose. Though sometimes displays are important, even a primary goal, most times you need to have the lowest possible profile. Your team members should rely on each other and no one else. You serve as each other's safety net. Never forget that fact.

Discuss your operation only with those people directly cleared by your client. Even if you suspect, by virtue of chain of command or relationship, that a person knows the details of your operation, keep your own counsel. Make every effort to avoid discussing the operation outside of a secure site. Because those who use electronic and magical eavesdropping techniques have reached new heights of subtlety and sophistication, you are automatically vulnerable anywhere outside your secure zone.

Create a secure zone. Your client may provide one for you as part of your contract, but you must take steps to ensure that it truly is secure. Supplement existing physical, electronic, and magical security with your own. Again, if your client is a professional, he'll understand the importance of this step to prevent problems and unwanted situations down the line.

Maintain weapon security. Operatives needlessly jeopardize countless operations by failing to maintain weapon security. Transport your weapons secretly and securely. Don't risk exposure by allowing a local to spot a concealed weapon. If you need to carry one for personal safety, be smart and discreet. Don't display your weapon, and don't use it as a badge of honor—it's not. It's a weapon. It kills people. Never forget what it is and why you carry it.

Once you are secure in your zone of operation, update your research. Use local resources to see if anything has changed since your initial research. For example, always check the terrain. Never assume that your map is accurate. Things change quickly in this day and age. Conduct reconnaissance, review your existing intelligence, update your plans, modify your procedures. Stay on top of the situation. You are in the zone; what was once paperwork and projections is now real. Your life is on the line.

>>>>>(Many mercs (and others) forget that situations are dynamic. Engrossed in their own plans, they forget that the opposition can and does react to events by taking action. The situation will change. The operative must forecast the change and move before it.)<<<<<
—Jade Horseman (17:25:06/11-12-55)

TYPES OF WORK

Mercs perform three main types of work: corp work, government work, and independent (indi) work. All merc operations share common elements, but significant differences distinguish these three types of work. The following descriptions provide an overview of common mercenary working conditions.

Corporate Work

Corporate work has become the mercenary's most reliable source of potential income, though available government work appears to be on an upswing, possibly in response to corp work. Corps most often hire mercs to supplement existing corp forces, either security or military. The most common assignment is simple site security, protecting a large or small facility. The area of operation is usually an unstable region that makes the corp nervous about the safety of its installation. Corps rarely create site-security assignments in a country or a major urban center administered by a stable government, preferring to devote their security resources to areas of unstable government or intense corporate competition.

Corporate work usually places mercs within the corporation's chain of command, where they must follow orders rather than giving them. Corporations often require their hired soldiers to do dirty work. If such work violates your personal code, stay away from corp assignments.

>>>>>(I've done a lot of these ops. You could say it's my forte. (I might say it too if I knew what the word meant.) Usually, the corp is expecting trouble, and so initially deploys you to some off-site location. They keep you there in a state of high readiness, and then sneak you on-site. If the opposition isn't paying attention (and they're usually too busy getting their own operation in motion to discover yours), they're caught by surprise. It works more often than you'd guess. Personally, I'd have laid bets that the opposition would be watching the site morning, noon, and night in every situation.)<<<<<
—Leaguer (12:09:28/01-13-55)

>>>>>(You'd be amazed.)<<<<<
—Hatchetman (21:29:17/01-16-55)

Corps rarely use mercs for internal security. Most often, mercenaries perform outside security at sites far removed from principal corporate enclaves.

Mercs supplementing corporate military forces usually work in hot spots. The corps don't hire mercs unless they expect trouble, and serious trouble only crops up in unstable regions. To the best of my knowledge, however, the corps don't recruit mercs for Desert Wars. If they do it at all, they do it quietly and hope the opposing corps and the networks don't find out.

Corps sometimes hire mercs for "face-offs," when two or more corps settle their differences by force of arms. This type of assignment sometimes takes the form of non-lethal, tag-gun combat, but sometimes it's high-pay hazard/lethal work.

>>>>>(Corporate military actions offer no joy. Corp forces are too well equipped. You can't protect yourself against half these weapons, and protection against the other half relies on some piece of barely substantial microtronic hardware. Really builds the old confidence, let me tell you.)<<<<<
—Worm Heart (22:39:27/01-14-55)

Government and Related Work

Mercs find government work easy to come by, and this work often provides long-term contracts. Governments, especially those of less prosperous and less stable nations, like to use mercs because mercenaries pro-

vide and manage their own assets. Most contracts include a replacement or reimbursement clause, which most governments find a more efficient and economical alternative than owning and maintaining the equipment themselves.

>>>>>(This is certainly the case for sophisticated electronics and such. For example, most developing countries contract at least half their air assets, usually more than half. Many also contract for radar and surveillance assets, as well as defensive surface-to-air systems and the like. Much more economical, at least until the systems need repair. And even then, most combat units assume partial liability for damage or loss.)<<<<<
     —Sten (21:10:14/01-11-55)

Government merc work tends to be high-mortality, however, because it relies heavily on garrison and area control duty in unstable regions, suppressing rebellions, and countering guerrilla warfare. Mercs performing government work must deal with high exposure: you move often and quickly, you rarely have time to secure a location, and the locals may act against you. Because these jobs offer the highest pay scale, that single advantage regularly outweighs the disadvantages. You takes the money and takes your chances.

Mercs may also receive offers of anti-government work, which pits them against mercs doing government work. Anti-government jobs tend to offer low pay and many dangers, but these types of assignments attract the altruistic mercs who can still believe in a cause. Though I have stated that I only take jobs I believe in, altruism is not part of my personal code. Altruism can blind you. A merc needs a pragmatic intellect to out-argue his emotions. If yours does not, I wish you well.

Indi Work

All the operations I've described so far offer opportunities to all-merc teams through established channels. A mercenary can also find work through independent channels. In plain English, I'm talking about so-called "shadowrunning" opportunities.

>>>>>(Yeah, all-merc teams—you know, buncha guys dressed like leaves sitting around in the woods coppin' a 'tude.)<<<<<
     —Wag (09:20:18/01-14-55)

A shadowrun puts a merc into a familiar yet different environment. In this kind of job, you become part of a multi-function team created to achieve some short-term goal. The task will require you to use all your skills in heavy exposure. You enter the operation as an individual rather than as part of an established team, though you may ultimately negotiate the terms of your contract as an individual or as part of the temporary group.

For nearly every shadowrun, you will have the best tactical skills in the group. You are there to offer the benefits of those skills. Everyone in the group has a niche, a specific role to play. Demand and maintain control of your area of expertise.

>>>>>(Hey, I always thought we hired the merc because he had the light machine gun?)<<<<<
     —Vambrace (21:29:14/01-15-55)

>>>>>(Shhhh, don't let him hear you. . .)<<<<<
     —Wedge (21:39:09/01-16-55)

One word of warning: indi employers (clients in the "shadowrunning" end of the business) generally hold poor opinions of shadowrunners. Why? Because shadowrunners rarely act like professionals, in our sense of the term. They have no personal discipline, no code, no sense of honor or trust, and no discretion. If you work as part of a "shadowrunning" team, it becomes more important than ever that you remain alert, smart, and professional. Someone has to.

>>>>>(See! What did I tell you!)<<<<<
     —Hatchetman (17:09:28/01-13-55)

>>>>>(So? You told us you'd read through the file once before posting.)<<<<<
     —Vulture Vic (03:41:51/01-14-55)

TYPES OF OPERATIONS

Everything you've read so far has explained what a mercenary should know about himself, his operation, and his opposition. This next section describes the standard types of merc operations. Each type involves unique peculiarities and concerns, and each could form the basis of an entire book. The best I can do with my limited space is to provide some food for thought.

In my opinion, the Desert Wars represent an insult to everything I hold true about my profession and cannot be included in a discussion of war in any sense.

>>>>>(Go Guards!)<<<<<
—Toiler (20:18:27/01-12-55)

>>>>>(Honestly, do you have any idea how many Desert War participants use some variation of the name "Guards"?!)<<<<<
—Houda (14:17:16/01-14-55)

OPEN WARFARE

The flat-out fight commonly seen in war trids and other such forms of entertainment represents the least common assignment a mercenary is likely to pick up these days, simply because no one is currently fighting the kind of wars in which standard armies clash with each other. That kind of war just doesn't happen any more. Occasional skirmishes take place between company-size units (100 men), but these rarely expand beyond border clashes or brushfire wars that flare up quickly and die just as quickly. The days of large-scale military clashes are past. Modern-day conflicts tend to take place between warlords, provinces, and relatively small forces. The Euro-Wars marked the end of true "warfare" in the classical sense.

>>>>>(What about the secession of Tir Tairngire from NAN? The way I read it certainly sounded like warfare in the sense he's talking about.)<<<<<
—Loodles (13:27:45/01-14-55)

>>>>>(Not the secession itself, but perhaps the Battle of Redding. That incident, of course, resulted from Tir forces entering northern California and engaging dug-in California National Guard units near Redding. Official versions of that engagement state that the Tir entered California with the equivalent of an armored division. That number might be exaggerated a bit, but no records try to dispute that the Tir mounted an extensive force. The short duration of the engagement makes it one of Matador's brushfire wars rather than open warfare. I should also point out that the Euro-Wars were still

in progress when this skirmish played out, which further reinforces Matador's statement.)<<<<<
—Colonel Cobra (11:10:15/11-15-55)

Will we see open warfare anytime soon? Not likely. If any such action does occur, ten to one it will involve Aztlan and the Confederated American States, a couple of the Russian satellites, or a few of the mid-African regimes.

Multitudes of books explain in mind-numbing detail how to fight a modern war. I see no point in retreading them here. If you have any interest in this field, you already know these books. I strongly recommend that you restrict your reading list to works published in this century and earlier by the following strategists: Sun Tzu, Clausewitz, Napoleon, Rommel, and Dunnigan. These works can provide insights that the current generation of modern electronic battlefield mavens could never hope to understand. No matter how expensive the gadgets, the basics remain the same.

GUERRILLA WARFARE

Guerrilla warfare currently best represents the realities of modern war. Small force versus large force. Rebel versus oppressor. Minority versus majority. Mercs usually find work on the side of the "majority," except in cases of externally financed insurrection, because the larger force usually has more resources. The smaller opposition, or the minority, usually lacks training but makes up for it in dedication and inspiration. Because they believe they have "right" on their side, the minority opponent is always dangerous.

I commented earlier in this book that anyone can fire a submachine gun into a crowd. The minority force represents the anyones. The farmers, the merchants, the men, the women, and even the children *believe* in their cause and will die for it. They might take you with them, if you're not careful.

Whether you believe in the side you're on is between you and your conscience. But it is important to realize that in such a conflict, both sides may be right. Always remember that conflicts rarely arise from simple issues. If people feel strongly enough to fight, the issue is important to them. Never dismiss your opponent's beliefs, because those beliefs are as valid as yours.

Guerrilla warfare is difficult. You fight an opponent who knows the terrain far better than you do, a motivated opponent who doesn't want you there. In guerrilla warfare, anything goes. Such fighting is never a gentlemen's war.

No matter what happens, no matter what they do, no matter how hard they push, you must never stoop to the opposition's level. Adhere to your rules of engagement. Abide by the original Geneva Conventions and the 2042 Munich Amendments. Fight honorably. Let them worry about sleeping at night.

>>>>>(Easy for you to say. People who hurt my people pay. That's my code.)<<<<<
—Stoneface Jackson (23:20:07/01-14-55)

>>>>>(Actually, it probably wasn't easy for him to say.)<<<<<
—Winter Rat (04:56:35/01-15-55)

Opponents in guerrilla warfare constantly try to force the other side to make mistakes, especially to harm civilians. If you feel any doubt about a civilian's guilt, err on the side of mercy. Do not attack a target that might include innocents. This stand gets tough, because the opposition tends to hide among the civilian population and dare you to strike. Don't take the dare; instead, make your own opportunities for battle. Be proactive in your stance and tactics. Force your opponents into the open. Force them into action by targeting the opposition leaders.

I can see your scowls already. You think that what I'm suggesting violates my code, the part that objects to assassination. Well, what of it?

Quite simply, I do not view a leader who chooses to hide his forces among the innocent as worth my compassion. He hides his soldiers among the local population *assuming* that his opponent will come after them and civilians will die. If such a leader really cared for his people, he would do everything in his power to protect them. Any other attitude demonstrates the workings of an evil mind. I suffer no compunction about assassinating such soulless men.

Assassinations and guerrilla warfare in general become more difficult to conduct against a truly partisan opponent, when your opponent *is* the civilian. History shows us that all conflicts fought against motivated civilians result in long, bloody struggles. Any time I see a conflict against civilians shaping up, I walk. No military solution exists in such situations, short of unrestricted warfare and genocide, and I will not participate in that kind of warfare.

>>>>>(You moral snob. That's right, pick and choose your fights. Only get involved in the clean fights, lest we dirty our khakis. Your pretentiousness and hypocrisy make me sick.)<<<<<
—Mother Maker (02:10:28/01-15-55)

>>>>>(Don't lose it on your keyboard. Half-digested soy-food and bile is a bear to clean out from between the keys.)<<<<<
—Mugger Hugger (10:28:27/01-16-55)

DISPLAYS

Displays provide a show of power to potential opposition. Your employers assume that your capable-looking presence at a location or function will deter any possible trouble. I believe that most displays fall into one of two categories: dress displays and field displays.

Dress displays are like Halloween. You dress up and play soldier. Your employer asks you to act as a "military advisor" for the evening at some military or quasi-military function that his adversaries will also attend. You talk a good game and convince your client's enemies that he, you, and "hundreds" like you mean business.

An employer might also ask you to appear in force and parade around. Some mercs love this kind of service, others hate it. If I can save a dozen lives by putting on my dress braids, it's a worthwhile effort. Other times, the same situation makes me feel like a puppet.

In a field display, a merc goes out in the field and gets noticed. Air-based mercenary units (chopper or fighter mercs) like this type of assignment especially well because they get paid simply for doing flybys and buzzing the crowd.

Unfortunately, a field display may quickly and unexpectedly become a skirmish. The warlord you've been hired to impress may decide to start shooting. If you take on a field display, include response and defense clauses in your contract, and a provision to re-negotiate if the situation changes. Always be ready to respond to a dynamic situation.

BUG HUNTS/"THE BIG GAME"

I include this employment opportunity simply because it has become a lucrative field for the single operator. This type of "assignment" places mercs as assistants to professional and not-so-professional hunters on animal-hunting excursions. You provide tactical advice and skilled, heavy weapon back-up should the client (usually a corp exec) fail to "bag the big one" before the "big one" tries to bag him.

Another phenomenon that attracts many mercs is "The Big Game," simsense producer Brilliant Genesis' game show/contest/ratings grabber. As you might expect, in this production famous (and not-so-famous) big-game hunters and mercs hunt big game, in this case defined as paranormal creatures. The show awards points for bagging different kinds of critters (no sentients accepted), with the scale sliding higher or lower depending on how dangerous the creature is and the weapons used to kill it. For example, killing a creature using an assault cannon when an assault rifle would have sufficed is worth fewer points, and using your fists when a rocket launcher is the standard weapon of choice is worth more.

Strange stuff. I don't endorse it or dismiss it, merely relate it.

>>>>>(Bagged me a pair of banshees (the elfie/howling kind). That'll knock my points way up there!)<<<<<
　　—Henry Hunter (21:08:29/11-14-55)

SECURITY

Security work can be fairly straightforward or may offer unpleasant complications. Because you work under a corporate overseer, the corp decides on tactics and procedures. How well the operation comes off depends on the competence of the corporate coordinator.

Though this subject deserves a full-length treatment, suffice it to say that corporate security work can be one of the safest types of assignments because inter-corporate conflicts rarely involve out-and-out destruction of assets. A merc working security might get hurt, but if your opponent is playing by the same rules, he's not shooting to kill.

PERSONAL SERVICE

Mercs who take personal service work usually serve several loosely defined functions; bodyguard, advisor, and dress display. A merc hired to perform personal service may become the client's confidant, co-conspirator, protection, threat display, and potential scapegoat. This difficult job tends to place you at the center of the maelstrom. You stand at the heart of a situation, at the focal point of all the machinations and passions, and closest to the truth. This perspective allows you to quickly determine the things that may not be as they seemed, and allows you to walk away early if necessary.

A merc can pick up this kind of work from a client living in fear who needs a protective presence to reassure him so that he can meet each new day. These people often have a very good reason to be afraid. Once you determine that reason, you must decide whether or not you want to continue working for this individual. Your decision marks who you are and what kind of work you will accept. Make your decisions carefully.

As you establish a reputation based on these decisions, you may develop long-lasting relationships with people who are or become important. In these cases, you may assume that you know the truth going in, or at least the truth as understood by the client. These leaders may come to rely on you to occasionally lend your expertise in more than one situation.

>>>>>(But be careful. Petty dictators find it easy to assign blame for failures to others. And you may be one of your client's few advisors that isn't a blood relative.)<<<<<
—Jooom (24:06:42/01-16-55)

As you gain experience and further your reputation, you may receive the opportunity to ascend almost to the top of the merc ladder and serve as an advisor.

ADVISORS

The most favorable position a merc can accept is that of an advisor. Your employers bring you in as a consulting expert in the military field, and so respect your opinion and listen to your advice. If your reports and their desires coincide, they may place you in a position of great power from which you command troops and recruit others farther down the professional mercenary ladder.

>>>>>(You make arrangements for the client, essentially becoming his fixer by using your fixer/dealer to get what's needed. A nice position to be in.)<<<<<
—Sten (18:28:14/01-16-55)

The lure of such power and influence may tempt you to tell your client what he or she wants to hear, regardless of the truth of the situation. By doing so, you virtually guarantee yourself continued employment.

Don't do it.

Always play it straight. If your research and expertise tells you one thing, don't tell the client something different. Give him the hard news. He may not thank you for it, but unless you are working in some dark corner of the planet devoid of all trappings of civilization, the days of killing the messenger are long gone. You might lose your job because you told him something he didn't want to hear, but when the drek hits the turbofan later down the road, someone might remember your evaluation and warning. Next time, they just might listen. And if that client won't, someone else may.

Most advisors receive excellent pay, topnotch support and accommodations, and mind-blowing perks. Don't allow yourself to be seduced. It's easy to fall victim to the luxury and forget why you are there, but remember that

other people will pay most dearly for your mistakes. If the policies you recommend fail, you might lose your job, but the dog soldiers in the field will pay the ultimate price.

SPECIAL OPERATIONS

Special ops, the black stuff, are performed by small units for high pay under very dangerous conditions. Killer work (so to speak) if you can get it, and the best of the best often do. Corps, governments, and many independent outfits run special ops, and mercs reap the benefits. It's difficult to know how many special ops are being run these days, because pros rarely talk about their work. There's no profit in bragging. The people who need to know what you've done in order to recommend you for another job always find out. You don't have to tell them.

>>>>>(Braggers tend to be floaters.)<<<<<
—Sanction (08:02:30/01-17-55)

Special ops covers an almost limitless range of assignments. You name it, and someone's probably been paid to do it. Extractions, kidnappings, hit-and-runs, search-and-destroys, anti-asset raids, harassment raids, infiltration and sabotage, commando work—all these and more fall under special operations.

Today, most special ops fall under the unfortunate heading of shadowrunning. If you want that work, you've got to work the streets. Some mercs refuse these offers, but most consider the work too lucrative to pass up. Mercs will find, however, that their expertise is under-appreciated in the shadowrunning market. Runners universally consider the merc nothing more than the guy with the big gun. You've got to teach them otherwise. Show them why they need a true professional in their midst.

>>>>>(I always insist on a professional in our midst, especially after a good fight. A professional masseuse, that is.)<<<<<
—Durango Jack (22:32:27/01-16-55)

>>>>>(You are a toad.)<<<<<
—Sheila Sunrise (08:20:16/01-18-55)

ORGANIZATIONS

The number of mercenary organizations has risen in the last twenty-odd years. Germany's MET 2000 group and associated assets represent the top tier. They sign mercs like you and me to long-term contracts, train them into units, then assign the units to contracts with clients. It's a sweet deal for a merc. You cut through all the planning and asset-managing to the job at hand and still get well paid. Not bad, eh?

The down side of belonging to a merc organization like MET 2000 is that such organizations make it extremely difficult to leave their ranks. You are working on the company's terms, living with a corporate rather than a personal code, and can no longer walk away if the situation changes for the worse. You are not in control—you are a company man. MET 2000 does not allow its employees to bail out of a contract, and the organization has an arm long enough to reach those who do.

>>>>>(Matador, you *goronit*, you hate MET 2000 because we skinned your hide last year. Admit it!)<<<<<
—MET 2000 Observer (04:20:19/01-13-55)

>>>>>(If you believe that's what happened, you're even more of a corporate toad than I thought.)<<<<<
—Matador (13:51:10/01-14-55)

Not every merc shares my point of view on this subject. In fact, a few thousand employees of MET 2000 would probably disagree with me. (By the way, don't blindly accept any published MET 2000 membership numbers. I have it on good authority that those numbers are grossly inflated.) I respect the choice of those who disagree with me. And for others who might find such indentured servitude desirable, I provide a short list of the better-known and financially respected international mercenary companies. Friends of mine have worked for these companies with what they consider desirable results.

MET 2000 (Germany)
BrightEdge (Morocco)
Tsunami (Japan/Far East)
10,000 Daggers (Constantinople)
Combat Inc. (Hong Kong)

THE LEAGUE

The League is a phenomenon that I can only describe as the international brotherhood of mercenaries. No formal organization, no meeting place, no dues, and no newsletter for the League exist. In fact, nothing exists to identify this group as a group. Yet all mercenaries are members of the League simply by virtue of their profession as soldiers of fortune.

All members of the League should treat each other with respect and fairness, as long as they deserve it. A fool who jeopardizes himself and others through idiotic posturing and ill-considered actions has lost his place in the brotherhood, and deserves only contempt.

The tradition of fair treatment especially applies to your opponent. Your opposite number took a job with the other side for the same reason you agreed to work for your side. Don't treat opposing mercenaries unfairly just because the conflict becomes ugly. Remember such sim-

ple niceties as respect and consideration, and others will show those qualities toward you.

>>>>>(Honestly, the drek these mercs dream up to keep themselves off the emotional hook. "I'm in the League so I don't have to suffer the incarceration and torture being inflicted on the regular troops I served with. Pass the tea please, will you?" Makes me vomit.)<<<<<
—Mother Maker (02:18:32/01-15-55)

MAGICAL INTEGRATION

Magic is so prevalent these days that I don't bother to make a distinction between standard and "mystical" assets. My attitude, however, remains unique. Corporations, especially, foolishly insist on grouping paranatural assets together and thinking of them as separate from their security or military assets.

Mercenaries use magic in every situation where it seems appropriate, but mostly to accomplish tasks as efficiently as possible. Magic is ideal for surveillance and recon work because it enables you to pick up a lot of information at low risk and low exposure. Magic also offers many advantages in anti-espionage work, securing your physical site, and protecting your own assets.

Magic has very little offensive value, simply because too few mages are in the field to wage effective magical warfare. Special ops regularly use mages to great effect, but magic offers few advantages to other operations. Employers sometimes attach a magician to a field ops unit, but only if the field unit has a specific objective that can be achieved most efficiently using magic. I personally know of only one or two units that permanently include a magician.

>>>>>(Again, what about the Tir secession from NAN? Seems like lots of combat magic went down there!)<<<<<
—Loodles (13:39:40/01-14-55)

>>>>>(Read the battle reports again, Loodles. My read is that the Tir used invisibility to conceal their forces. It was 2036; if the CNC weren't concerned enough about such possibilities to guard against them, then they got what was coming to them. On the other hand, I suspect that all the tales of combat magic from those battles were somewhat exaggerated.)<<<<<
—Colonel Cobra (11:46:04/11-15-55)

When a magician takes part in an operation, he should be deployed as a special weapons team and sent where needed. Currently, magicians primarily fill recon and defensive roles. I suspect those roles will someday change, but most likely not until long after I leave the business.

HOT SPOTS

I've covered the why and how and who of being a mercenary. The following list tells you where. The world situation is too volatile for any list to be comprehensive, but the places described below represent the current government/anti-government hot spots. For any other kind of work, buy an atlas and mark all the megacities. Be sure to say hello if you see me out there.

AZTLAN

Today, right now, Aztlan offers one of the biggest markets for anti-government work in the merc biz. The rebel forces enjoy generous financial backing, so Aztlan work tends to pay well.

The Azzies are a brutal people and highly skilled at war. They pride themselves on self-sufficiency, which means they don't care for mercenaries and so treat them poorly. Because the Aztlan problem is effectively a civil war with external backers, both sides can draw from a large pool of guerrilla warriors, but these enthusiastic soldiers lack training. Mercs act as trained leaders and advisors, making ripe targets for the opposition.

FAR EAST

Southeast Asia remains a mess. Since the Awakening, virtually all political borders have disappeared. Only Korea maintains any semblance of cohesion, and even that nation seems fragile these days. Warlords dominate, and mercs abound. The Far East is a dangerous, changing environment controlled by leaders with no morals and few concerns beyond their petty dictatorships. The pay is good, but the risks are high.

AUSTRALIA

A decent amount of merc work exists in Australia, mainly protecting supply caravans and enclaves against local and preternatural forces. The pay is good, but the wildness of the region, especially the rampant magic, is not for the faint of heart.

AFRICA

Unfortunately, present-day Africa is a mecca for merc work. Small nation-states or city-states and their warlords employ countless mercs to sort out their internal upheavals. As in Southeast Asia, the region brims over with chaos and danger. But if you didn't thrive on those conditions, you'd have stopped reading this screed long ago.

THE END OF THE MERCENARY

The battlefield is changing. As I've pointed out, precious few people still fight all-out wars. Few nations or corps have or are willing to spend the vast financial resources needed for such a venture. As always, manpower is cheap but the tools of warfare are not. Subterfuge, espionage, and counterespionage have replaced armies of tanks as the tools for solving national problems.

This is good.

Sure, ultimately it means less work for me, but it also means fewer threats to life and limb for everyone else. I'd rather see the world's problems resolved with small skirmishes, police actions, and brushfire wars. Better that than the alternative.

What does this mean for my profession? It means we must adapt. I believe that future battles will be fought by small units wielding incredibly sophisticated weapons capable of focusing more firepower than you or I can even imagine, and magic will also play an important part. I foresee that the soldier of the future will be part mage, part mercenary, and part metal.

Mercs like us won't be part of that battlefield.

We will still be part of the battlefield where the real people fight. We'll be where people bleed, and hurt, and fight for causes they believe in. We'll be standing next to them, waiting for the charge.

Maybe I'll see you there.

>>>>>(Don't count on it.)<<<<<
—Smiley (21:17:17/01-04-55)

MERCENARY EQUIPMENT

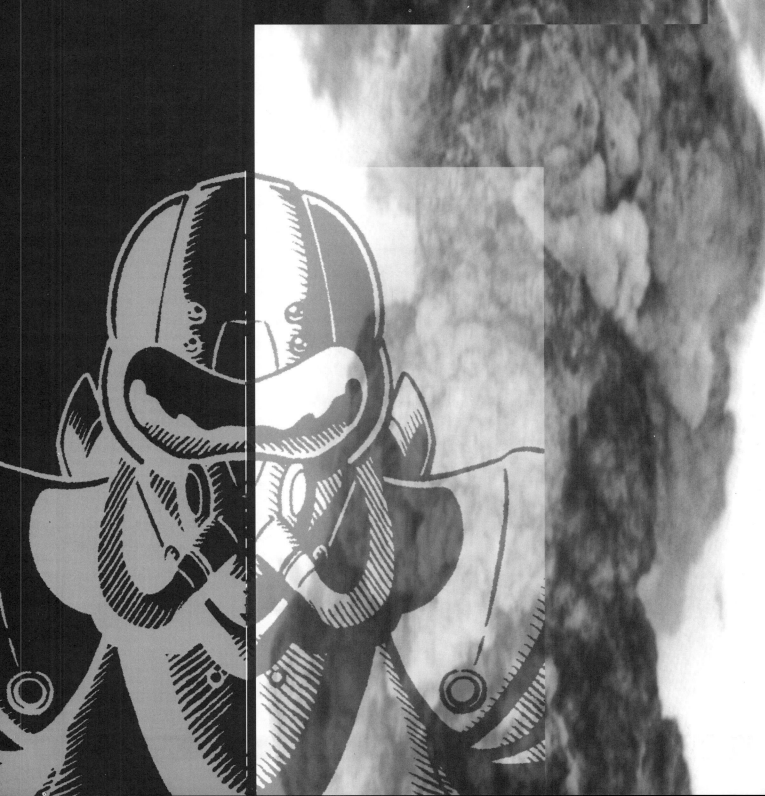

WALTHER PB-120

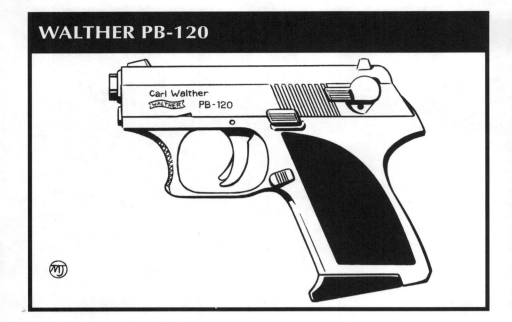

SALESPERSON

In the field, reliability means everything. The Walther PB-120 offers total reliability in a low-profile, easy-to-hide, back-up pistol. Constructed primarily of composite materials, the light but rugged PB-120 works like a charm even in the most hostile environment. A merc couldn't ask for a better piece.

In addition to the standard 10-shot clip, Walther also produces a 15-shot, extended clip for emergency situations. Despite its small size, the weapon can mount standard barrel and top-mounted accessories made by most manufacturers.

Type	Conceal	Ammo	Mode	Damage	Weight	Availability	Cost	Street Index
Light	8 (6)	10 (15) (c)	SA	6L	.75	6/36	700¥	2

This weapon cannot accept under-barrel accessories.

>>>>>(This gun has always impressed me: I've carried it as my primary back-up for five years now. Good solid performer, light and easy to handle. Gets my vote.)<<<<<
    —Matador(10:18:14/8-10-54)

>>>>>(Yeah, but the light load scrags it for me. Why pack something that can barely scratch a rabbit?)<<<<<
    —Catcher (08:14:41/8-20-54)

>>>>>(Scratch a rabbit? Remind me to stay away from the places you frequent. Yikes.)<<<<<
    —Crayfish (20:51:17/8-22-54)

>>>>>(Catcher, do what I do: pack explosive APDS rounds. If you hit that rabbit, there ain't gonna be much left of it.)<<<<<
    —Matador (08:29:27/9-02-54)

>>>>>(Oh, like it's easy to find exploding APDS. I'll just jander down to the Shini-Walgreens. . .)<<<<<
    —Vandal (20:29:13/9-14-54)

>>>>>(Get some. Keep the edge.)<<<<<
    —Sanction (00:10:29/9-15-54)

HAMMERLI MODEL 610S

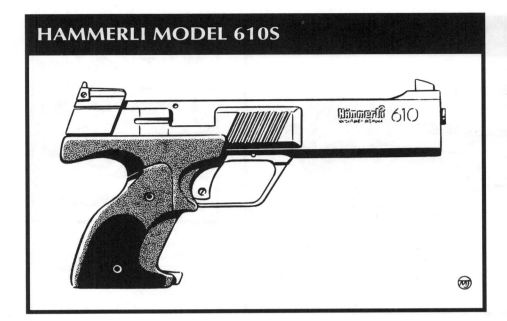

SALESPERSON

Designed as a match-target weapon, the Hammerli Model 610s makes a powerful and effective personal sidearm. A stylish weapon, the Model 610s is the first choice of a marksman and a true soldier. First class all the way!

Designed to minimize muzzle jump and vibration, customizable grip pads and weights allow the individual user to configure his weapon for maximum comfort and balance. The simple quick-lock system is fully compatible with a variety of top-mounted accessories, and the Hammerli also boasts a patented gas-escape system.

Type	Conceal	Ammo	Mode	Damage	Weight	Availability	Cost	Street Index
Heavy*	4	6 (c)	SA	6L	2.5	8/24	1,295¥	2.5

*Though technically a light pistol, this target weapon uses the Heavy Pistol Range Table. For customization information, see **Rules**, p. 73. This weapon offers the equivalent of 1 point of Recoil Reduction, and cannot accept under-barrel or barrel-mounted accessories.

>>>>>(Like I'm going to pack a gun like this. Please, kill me now.(Looks wiz, though.))<<<<<
    —Rabid Fire
        (20:10:23/9-20-54)

>>>>>(Personal sidearm, sure. A field weapon it's not. I recommend it for dress duty. It looks deadly, and if you look like you know how to use it, you might not have to.)<<<<<
    —Colonel Cobra
        (02:16:48/9-29-54)

>>>>>(You lost me. "Dress duty?" And don't tell me it goes well with my little black cocktail number.)<<<<<
    —Tiger Lilly
        (06:39:29/10-10-54)

>>>>>(Uniform duty. High-profile operations where your presence is a deterrent, like bodyguard and protection where you need a tough look to scare people off. The silver and matte-black version does go well with most cocktail and evening dresses.)<<<<<
    —Colonel Cobra
        (01:11:40/10-12-54)

SAVALETTE GUARDIAN

SALESPERSON

The Savalette Guardian's chrome-steel finish shows off the taste of the true professional, and its high-powered, full-load slug packs professional power. This second-to-none pistol fires the heaviest round in its class. The Guardian's brilliant finish, integral computer-enhanced targeting system, micro-gyro recoil absorption system, and burst-mode firing system make this weapon the unquestioned leader of the pack. Whether field or dress weapon, the Savalette Guardian is the heavy sidearm of choice for professionals worldwide. Why pick any other gun?

Type	Conceal	Ammo	Mode	Damage	Weight	Availability	Cost	Street Index
Heavy	5	12 (c)	SA/BF	9M	3.25	6/36	900¥	2.5

Comes with an integral smartgun link. The Guardian offers the equivalent of 1 point of Recoil Reduction and can fire a single, three-round burst as a Complex Action. The weapon accepts all standard barrel and top-mounted accessories, but cannot mount under-barrel accessories.

>>>>>(Why pick another gun? 'Cause I ain't payin' nearly 2K for a fraggin' pistol! Especially one I can see myself in!)<<<<<
 —Flapjack
  (04:20:10/8-20-54)

>>>>>(Add up the cost of accessories. Say 400¥ for the weapon, double for the smartlink, then add another 400¥ for the recoil reduction. That's 1,200¥ and we ain't even got to the burst feature. The pup is worth it.)<<<<<
 —Toad (20:14:18/8-24-54)

>>>>>(Word of warning: I've had some problems with the smartlink. Twice now it's lost signal after it got jostled. Only for a moment, but long enough to cause real trouble.)<<<<<
 —Wolfman Al
  (19:13:29/9-02-54)

>>>>>(Sure it wasn't just your particular weapon?)<<<<<
 —Nay-sayer
  (08:41:10/9-03-54)

>>>>>(Nope. I replaced my first one, and a friend had a similar problem.)<<<<<
 —Wolfman Al
  (20:13:34/9-05-54)

INGRAM WARRIOR-10

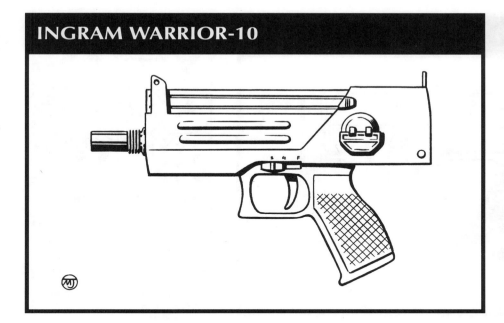

SALESPERSON

More Ingram Warrior-10s have sold in the past three years than some of its major competitors have sold in their entire product lives. Durable and reliable, the Warrior-10 is the weapon to choose when the elements are your enemy. Rain, sand, mud, humidity—under any conditions, the Warrior-10 keeps firing. No bells and whistles on this tough gun, but who cares about chrome when the rock-and-roll goes down?

Type	Conceal	Ammo	Mode	Damage	Weight	Availability	Cost	Street Index
SMG	4	30 (c)	SA/BF	7M	3	3/24	650¥	.9

The Ingram Warrior-10 can mount all barrel, under-barrel, and top-mounted accessories.

COLT COBRA

SALESPERSON

Everyone who's ever seen tridvids like *Fireteam Cherokee* knows the Colt Cobra by its distinctive silhouette. It's the best submachine-gun on the market today, and not just on trideo. Bench-test it against any other make or model; none of them can match the Cobra's accuracy or repeatability. Special-weapons units around the globe use the Cobra as their standard SMG: the basic TZ-110 model with its barrel-integrated gas-venting system, the TZ-115 with a built-in laser sight, or the TZ-118 with a built-in smartlink. Do what the world's top guns do: pack a Cobra.

Type	Conceal	Ammo	Mode	Damage	Weight	Availability	Cost	Street Index
SMG	5	32 (c)	SA/BF/FA	6M	3	6/36	700¥	2

Colt Cobra TZ-110 comes with a folding stock standard and an integral Gas-Vent II system that offers Recoil Reduction (1). The TZ-115 model comes with integral laser sight for 850¥; the TZ-118 comes with integral smartlink for 1,000¥. All models accept standard under-barrel and top-mounted accessories, but cannot accept barrel-mounted accessories.

>>>>>(Despite what they say about the Warrior-10, I've seen more and more Cobras lately. These days I expect to see it, especially in corp territory.)<<<<<
　　—Seeker
　　　(21:23:48/10-15-54)

>>>>>(If you see a particular weapon in the hands of regular corp forces, odds are the corps are using it in bulk. The corps work like the military that way; once they choose a weapon, they buy and distribute it in bulk. Makes maintenance and repair easier if everyone is using the same gun.)<<<<<
　　—Trader Vic
　　　(03:20:41/10-19-54)

>>>>>(And when a big corp trades up to a new model, the secondary markets (read: shadow) are flooded with the old weapons at a discount. Used, of course.)<<<<<
　　—Dented Fred
　　　(22:10:32/10-22-54)

>>>>>(I hear the UCAS Army is gonna pick these up.)<<<<<
　　—Snail (05:49:23/10-25-54)

INGRAM SUPER MACH 100

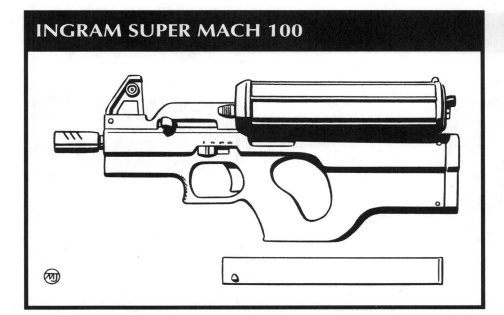

SALESPERSON

Pull the trigger and feel the power! Technically classified as a "super-machinegun," the Ingram SuperMach 100 has a patented firing system that offers controlled six-round bursts and a full-autofire rate that'll leave you breathless. It fires as fast as a minigun, without the recoil!

The SuperMach 100 uses both a standard 40-round clip and a special 60-round, high-density clip. Distinctive in appearance and sound, the SuperMach 100 gives the maximum bang for the nuyen.

Type	Conceal	Ammo	Mode	Damage	Weight	Availability	Cost	Street Index
SMG	5 (4)	40 (60)	(c)SA/BF/FA	6L	3 (3.25)	9/48	850¥	3

The SuperMach 100 fires Light Pistol rounds with the equivalent of 3 points of Recoil Reduction. In burst mode, it fires six-round bursts that do 12S damage, and has a maximum autofire rate of 15 rounds. Apply recoil modifiers as for normal rounds. The weapon accepts under-barrel and top-mounted accessories. An empty, 60-round clip costs 25¥.

>>>>>(I love this chica! The lead stream almost never stops; I can practically see it! And oh, what it does to what it hits. It makes me so happy.)<<<<<
—Tee-Hee
(12:05:36/9-23-54)

>>>>>(As long as your target is made of paper. Any kind of hardened target shrugs off these rounds with hardly a scratch. Too light for my tastes; give me the Ares HVAR any day.)<<<<<<
—Whisper
(02:02:19/9-26-54)

>>>>>(Definitely the HVAR—provided you can get away with slinging an assault rifle. What happens when you need a little subtlety?)<<<<<
—Findler-Man
(11:28:35/9-30-54)

>>>>>(Subtlety? Whisper? Oh, that's ripe. Bravo, Findler-Man!)<<<<<
—Steel Lynx
(21:28:09/10-02-54)

>>>>>(Choke me.)<<<<<
—Whisper
(03:01:38/10-03-54)

COLT M-23 ASSAULT RIFLE

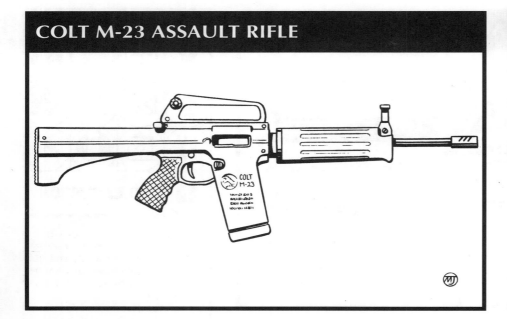

SALESPERSON

An army needs ordnance, and ordnance requires cash. If money's tight, a little cash needs to go a long way. The Colt M-23 assault rifle, a stripped-down version of the highly successful Colt M-22A2, is the ideal solution for the soldier on a budget. A powerful, capable weapon, the M-23 accepts all secondary accessories. Firepower now, expandable later, and no need to compromise!

Type	Conceal	Ammo	Mode	Damage	Weight	Availability	Cost	Street Index
Assault	3	40 (c)	SA/BF/FA	8M	4.5	6/36	950¥	2

The Colt M-23 assault rifle can mount standard barrel, under-barrel, and top-mounted accessories.

>>>>>(A popular weapon, especially on the streets. I've seen it in the hands of gangers, underworld thugs, shadowrunners, you name it. Why do they need bells and whistles?)<<<<<
—Condor
(08:20:38/9-25-54)

>>>>>(Developing-world and quasi-corporate weapon dealers have picked up the M-23 and other weapons in bulk and are selling them in the inner cities at an inflated price. Keep that in mind next time your fixer picks up an assault rifle for you on the cheap.)<<<<<
—Findler-Man
(11:32:14/9-30-54)

>>>>>(Are you objecting to the sale of weapons in the inner city, or the price-gouging?)<<<<<
Facer 'X'
(02:09:30/10-02-54)

>>>>>(Everyone should take care with shadow-market weapons. The ones that look chip-truth are often mini-industry manufacturing knock-offs; precision and reliability go down the sewer.)<<<<<
—Eve Donovan
(12:26:49/10-08-54)

ARES ALPHA COMBAT GUN

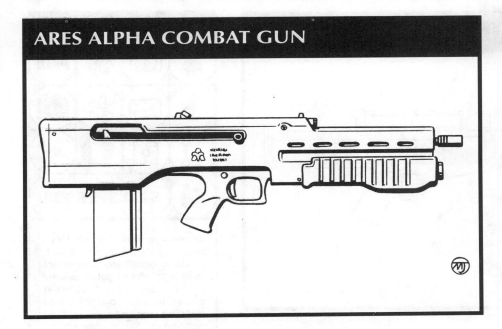

SALESPERSON

The weapon of choice for the upcoming decade, the Alpha Combatgun is the first of Ares Arms' two entries into the hotly contested battle rifle market. A precision weapon designed for special-forces operations, the Alpha Combatgun's integrated, full-function Smartlink Level II™ and high-speed data bus give it a responsiveness no other weapon can match. An integral mini-grenade launcher, chamber-based recoil-reduction, and Ares reliability makes the Alpha a weapon of unparalleled artistry.

Type	Conceal	Ammo	Mode	Damage	Weight	Availability	Cost	Street Index
Assault	2	42 (c)	SA/BF/FA	8M	5.25	18/48	2,000¥	4
Grenade	—	8 (m)	SS	Spec.	—	—	—	—

Comes with integral Smartlink II circuitry and an under-barrel mini-grenade launcher. The Alpha can accept barrel- and top-mounted accessories, but not under-barrel accessories. It offers the equivalent of 2 points of Recoil Reduction.

>>>>>(The Alpha has been making the rounds for a couple of years now, ever since Ares quietly distributed prototypes called the CAR-32 to "selected field-testers" and integrated their feedback into the production model. It seems they ignored one joker's request to integrate an under-barrel combat laser.)<<<<<
—Colonel Cobra
(12:05:26/11-15-54)

>>>>>(Speaking of that, I keep hearing that Ares is closer to a mass-production model of the man-portable laser system (formally the MP-CLS 100). Anybody else hear anything? The original came out four years ago.)<<<<<
—Wolfman Al
(05:45:47/11-19-54)

>>>>>(You spoke too soon, Wolfman Al. Check out the heavy weapon section of this file.)<<<<<
—Steel Lynx
(20:13:18/11-21-54)

>>>>>(Oh, my.)<<<<<
—Vandal
(10:20:38/11-22-54)

>>>>>(Better have a fat credstick, chummer.)<<<<<
—Steel Lynx
(21:02:02/11-24-54)

ARES HIGH-VELOCITY ASSAULT RIFLE

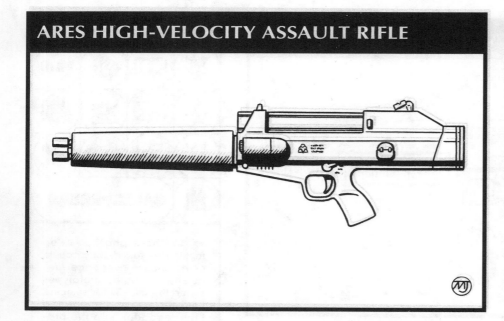

SALESPERSON

At last—the assault rifle that fires as fast as a super-machinegun! Ares Arms' latest assault rifle combines the top performance you expect from Ares with minigun firing rates for a rock-and-roll rifle beyond the pale and beyond belief!

The Ares Arms HVAR comes with patented Smartlink Level II™ technology that provides outstanding basic targeting and compensation algorithms designed to compensate for the weapon's unique features. The weapon package includes integral recoil reduction systems that offer enhanced stability even in full-fire mode! Suppression or covering fire with the HVAR lets the opposition know you mean business!

Type	Conceal	Ammo	Mode	Damage	Weight	Availability	Cost	Street Index
Assault	2	50 (c)	SA/BF/FA	6M	5.0	14/7 days	3,200¥	4

The Ares HVAR fires Light Pistol rounds. In burst mode it fires six-round bursts that do 12D damage at a maximum autofire rate of 15 rounds. The weapon comes with an integrated Smartlink II that offers the equivalent of 3 points of Recoil Reduction; apply recoil modifiers as for normal weapons. The HVAR accepts under-barrel and top-mounted accessories.

>>>>>(Now we're talking. I was working down in South America (won't say where) not long ago, when I got to use my HVAR. Laid myself down a cover screen so tight I was popping caps as soon as they hopped up. Nasty work, chummers, but I get paid well to do it.)<<<<<
—Whisper
(02:30:20/9-26-54)

>>>>>(Ya know, Whisper, I looked at the ballistic files on the HVAR after reading your comment about penetration. I got bad news for you: The HVAR don't penetrate much better than the SuperMach 100 you chucked a couple of screens back.)<<<<<
—Steel Lynx
(21:32:30/10-02-54)

>>>>>(You looking for trouble, Lynx? Want to start something? Everywhere I look, I find you cracking on me. You wanna play, we'll play, but by *my* rules.)<<<<<
—Whisper
(03:03:20/10-03-54)

>>>>>(Guess Morocco did wreck you after all.)<<<<<
—Steel Lynx
(10:20:14/10-05-54)

BARRET MODEL 121 HEAVY SNIPER RIFLE

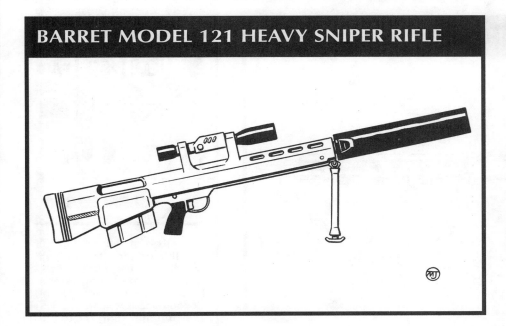

SALESPERSON

For the times when a standard round doesn't cut it, pick up the Barret Model 121 heavy sniper rifle and its custom, armor-piercing ammo. The heaviest small-arms round available, Barret ammo works against both soft and hard targets. Don't let armor skin slow you down; punch through it and take down your target.

The Model 121's integral silencer system combines with blow-back recoil compensation to give it precision balance in spite of its heavy caliber. Silent, deadly, and accurate, the Barret guarantees you one shot and one down.

Type	Conceal	Ammo	Mode	Damage	Weight	Availability	Cost	Street Index
Sniper	—	14 (c)	SA	14D	10	14/30 days	4,800¥	5

This weapon offers the equivalent of 2 points of Recoil Reduction and has a +2 recoil modifier. It also comes with an integral Smartlink I system. Treat custom ammo as APDS rounds; the ammo costs 200¥ per box of 10, and has the same Availability and Street Index as the weapon. A player must make separate tests to acquire each box.

>>>>>(Grade A+ bang-bang! This one's a frightening piece of work. An "associate" of mine uses the Model 121 extensively. I've backed her up on a couple of jobs; when she's fired at anything further away than a couple of meters, I've heard no gun noise whatso-ever. Scary.)<<<<<
—Hatchetman
(03:20:45/10-05-54)

>>>>>(You can use the Model 121 right out of the box; I had to use it that way once. I've upgraded mine to use Smartlink II hardware and fire caseless ammo: no casings, no evidence. The Smartlink's rangefinder makes the long shot a breeze. One drawback, though; the weapon doesn't come apart easily. You have to carry it assembled, and the fraggin' thing is almost as long as I am tall.)<<<<<
—Nightmare
(12:19:38/10-08-54)

>>>>>(Have you ever seen one of the slugs it fires?? I use them as paperweights.)<<<<<
—Toad (23:08:25/10-12-54)

REMINGTON 990 SHOTGUN

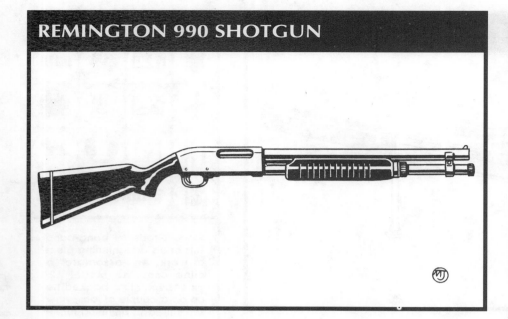

SALESPERSON

One of the world's most common shotguns, the Remington 990 plays a variety of roles. Security specialists, law enforcement, and field and site mercenary units favor the 990 as the ultimate simple, all-purpose shotgun. Years of service have proven the 990 a winner at an affordable price.

Type	Conceal	Ammo	Mode	Damage	Weight	Availability	Cost	Street Index
Shotgun	2	8 (m)	SA	See below*	4	3/48 hrs	650¥	2

*The 990 can fire slug or shot rounds (see p. 95, **SRII**) that do 8S or 10S damage. For a sawed-off version, increase Concealability to 4 and reduce all Damage Codes by –2.

>>>>>(Lots of security forces use this cannon to fire gel rounds, because it can switch between those non-lethal loads and more damaging standard loads with no trouble. The optional sling makes it easy to handle, and it never fails. I've staked my life on it.)<<<<<
—SPD (10:20:23/9-29-54)

>>>>>(I got my first Remington scattergun when I was 10. My dad spent days deciding exactly which model to buy for me. He tried them out, asked around, and finally decided on the 900 in matte black. I used it until last year, when I lost it in Aztlan. Ah, well.)<<<<<
—Matador (21:19:23/10-18-54)

>>>>>(I can just see you: sitting out on the back porch with yer scattergun, splattin' those barn varmints when they crawl out at night. Yep, yep. You are the NRA. Gimme some hay to chew, will ya, Ma?)<<<<<
—Crayfish (08:35:48/10-21-54)

>>>>>(I lived in Philadelphia, you beetle-head. If I thought for a minute you had a brain in your head, I'd splatter it.)<<<<<
—Matador (08:48:37/10-22-54)

FRANCHI SPAS-22

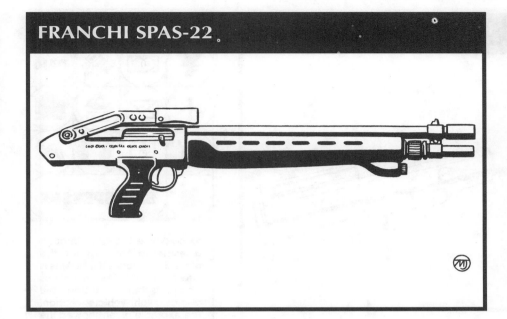

SALESPERSON

The latest in a long line of renowned combat shotguns, the SPAS-22 meets the most stringent performance standards. Capable of selective fire in both single-action and burst-fire modes, the SPAS-22 can hold its own at any time, in any place. A custom folding stock* lets it close up small, making it an ideal weapon for low-profile operations. The SPAS-22 comes with Smartlink II™ hardware, making an already outstanding weapon top gun the world over.

Type	Conceal	Ammo	Mode	Damage	Weight	Availability	Cost	Street Index
Shotgun	2 (4)	10 (m)	SA/BF	10S	4	6/48 hrs	1,000¥	2

*When folding stock is extended, the SPAS-22 offers the equivalent of 1 point of Recoil Reduction. The weapon has a +2 recoil modifier.

>>>>>(I love the SPAS-22 even more than the Mossberg CMDT. Feels more stable, fits my grip better, and so on. I especially like to use it in close quarters.)<<<<<
—Washer
(06:28:49/10-18-541)

>>>>>(The first combat shotguns were designed for house-to-house fighting and for combat in dense foliage, where you might need to punch through leaves, light woods, wallboard, and so on. The weapons still serve the same purpose.)<<<<<
—Colonel Cobra
(20:31:34/10-20-54)

>>>>>(?? I can punch through stuff, but if my target's hiding behind a wall or something, odds are I won't hit him!)<<<<<
—Flapjack
(04:20:39/10-21-54)

>>>>>(So? Punch holes in the wall, you moron!)<<<<<
—Toad (11:58:20/10-23-54)

ARES HV MP-LMG

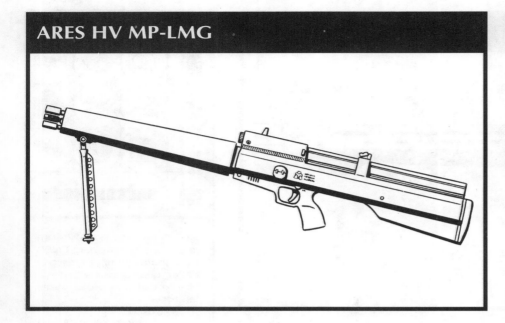

SALESPERSON

This second entry in Ares' high-velocity product line is a super-machinegun version of their popular man-portable, light machinegun. Designed to work as a personal weapon or a light or heavy mounted weapon, the HV MP-LMG is ideal for area control, especially when belt-fed from an independent source. As with other high-velocity models, the HV MP-LMG comes with an integrated Smartlink Level II; this top-notch computer interface makes for outstanding performance.

Type	Conceal	Ammo	Mode	Damage	Weight	Availability	Cost	Street Index
LMG	—	80 (c)	SA/BF/FA	6S	8.0	20/14 days	4,500¥	4

The Ares HV MP-LMG fires Light Pistol rounds at the equivalent of 3 points of Recoil Reduction. Apply recoil modifiers as for normal weapons. In burst mode, it fires six-round bursts that do 15D damage at a maximum autofire rate of 15 rounds. The weapon comes with an integrated Smartlink II and accepts under-barrel and top-mounted accessories.

>>>>>(While browsing through a restricted Ares catalog the other day, I noticed that Ares is offering the HV LMG not only as part of its Sentry™ system, but also as a light-vehicle weapon. The example given showed the weapon mounted on the Northrup Yellowjacket PRC-44F. Once they field that puppy, I'm going to be very upset.)<<<<<
—Findler-Man
(05:13:59/10-17-54)

>>>>>(Northrup started shipping the F upgrade package sixteen days ago. You'll find an entry for the package in a later file. Though no one says so, you can blame Saeder-Krupp for the gel-composite armor. Thank the dragon.)<<<<<
—Devious
(09:32:20/10-19-54)

>>>>>(Back to the HV LMG, I still think that super-machineguns, including bigger miniguns, are next to useless as man-portable weapons. Too much recoil, too little control. As vehicle-mounted or stationary weapons, they work great.)<<<<<
—Pullman Beak
(08:20:30/10-22-54)

M79B1 LIGHT ANTI ARMOR WEAPON

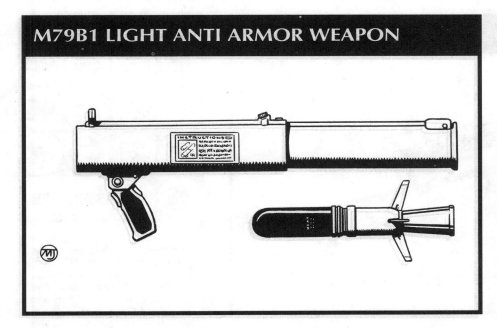

The M79B1 Light Anti-armor Weapon (LAW) is the most common weapon of its type in the world. Designed as a disposable, telescoping container, the single-shot LAW is self-contained and cannot accept accessories. Cheap but reliable, the LAW enables its user to take on almost any armored vehicle!

Fired from a shoulder mount, the LAW vents launch gases through the rear of the firing tube, virtually eliminating recoil. A simple, non-adjustable aperture permits excellent sighting under standard environmental conditions.

Type	Conceal	Ammo	Mode	Damage	Weight	Availability	Cost	Street Index
Missile	4/—*	1	SS	12D	2.5	6/36	700¥	2

*Telescoping container can only be fired when fully opened, reducing Concealability to 0. Firing requires a Complex Action.

Use the standard rocket rules for this weapon, p. 99, **SRII**. This weapon cannot accept accessories. The rocket does 12D Damage, reducing the Power of its blast by −1 for every half-meter, and is subject to scatter of 2D6 + 2. The LAW rocket is not compatible with a standard AVR launcher and does not have armor-piercing capability. A 1 x 10-meter blast zone behind the weapon is subject to 10M exhaust blast, reduced by −1 per meter.

>>>>>(The LAW isn't anti-armor if you're talking about tanks. It might punch a small hole in some light tanks, especially security vehicles, but it'll barely scratch anything with real armor.)<<<<<
—Hatchetman
(02:20:03/10-12-54)

>>>>>(Yeah, but it's only meant to take out light fortifications and lightly armored vehicles. For real anti-tank capability, upgrade to a true AVR or AVM. Course, you'd better have deep pockets.)<<<<<
—Mongoose
(05:13:19/10-19-54)

>>>>>(Yes, but a half-trained soldier with an AVM can take out a light or medium tank at a cost of less than 5K¥ for the dog. The tank plus training for its crew costs at least a hundred times that much. The AVM's well worth the investment.)<<<<<
—Colonel Cobra
(12:36:49/10-22-54)

>>>>>(Ever tried getting close enough to a Stonewall or Centurion to use a LAW? Thought not.)<<<<<
—Dog Boy
(21:23:58/10-24-54)

ARBELAST II MEDIUM ANTI ARMOR WEAPON

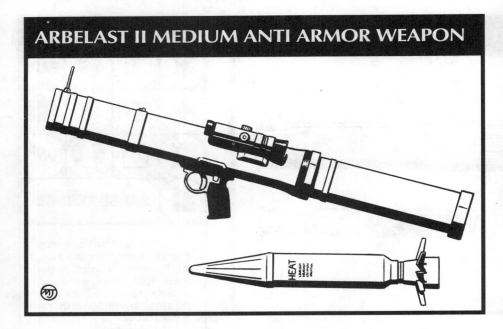

A heavier version of the LAW, the Arbelast II Medium Anti-armor Weapon (MAW) fires a heavier rocket and warhead. Unlike the LAW, the MAW's disposable firing canister does not telescope. The weapon includes a permanent, fixed-magnification system and secondary "pop-up" hard sights.

Type	Conceal	Ammo	Mode	Damage	Weight	Availability	Cost	Street Index
Missile	—	1	SS	15D	2.75	8/48	1,200¥	2

Use the standard rocket rules for this weapon, p. 99, **SRII**. This weapon cannot accept accessories. The rocket warhead does 15D Damage, reducing the Power of its blast by –1 for every half-meter, and is subject to Scatter of 2D6 + 2. The MAW rocket is not compatible with a standard AVR launcher and does not have armor piercing capability. A 1 x 12-meter blast zone behind the weapon is subject to 12M exhaust blast, reduced by –1 per meter.

>>>>>(Continuing Dog Boy's comment under the LAW entry, if you stand within an MBT's primary anti-personnel zone, you're worm food. Both the LAW and the MAW have a range of 1,500 meters, well outside the APZ. But neither the LAW nor the MAW can penetrate MBT armor, so the point is moot.)<<<<<
        —Colonel Cobra
                (05:12:54/10-26-54)

>>>>>(If you have the patience and take the time to to aim, LAWs and MAWs work great against low-flying aircraft. You probably won't hit your target, but *they* don't know that. They see the heat signature and the smoke trail, so they jink away. If they've got *cojones* they'll take the time to check their displays for locking or tracking first, but most don't.)<<<<<
        —Matador
                (06:13:49/10-29-54)

>>>>>(If you're smart, you set up a kill zone where you and another chummer have LAWs and a third has a SAM. You fire and the bird jinks away from you; the other LAW fires and the bird jinks again, right into the path of the SAM. Gotta love it.)<<<<<
        —Uncle SAM
                (08:20:10/10-30-54)

GREAT DRAGON ATGM

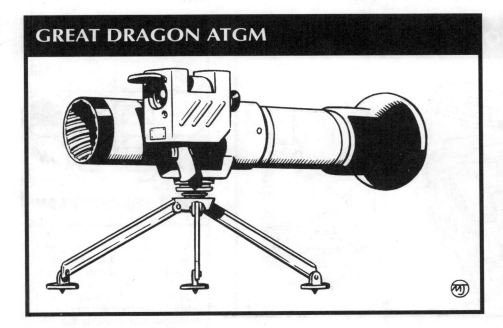

SALESPERSON

Co-manufactured by Mitsubishi and General Motors Military Division, the Great Dragon ATGM (anti-tank guided missile) is a ground-based spinoff of GM's popular Bandit air-to-ground missiles. Fired from a tripod-mounted, reusable canister, the Great Dragon ATGM has proven an effective battlefield weapon. An integral, semi-smart tracking system keeps the launched missile on target, and delayed main-engine ignition helps hide the launcher's location. These features, combined with a shaped-charge, armor-piercing warhead, enable the Great Dragon to stop enemy armor of any size.

Type	Conceal	Ammo	Mode	Damage	Weight	Availability	Cost	Street Index
L-ATGM	4	1	SS	20D	2.75	8/48	1,200¥	2

*See the Weapon Range Table, p. 87.

This weapon uses the standard missile rules, p. 99, **SRII**. This weapon cannot accept accessories, and includes a fixed Optical Magnification II sighting system. The armor-piercing missile warhead does 20D Damage, reducing the Power of its blast by –5 Blast per meter, and is subject to Scatter of 2D6. A 1 x 12-meter blast zone behind the weapon is subject to 12M exhaust blast, reduced by –1 per meter.

>>>>>(It can "stop any size of enemy armor?" Hardly. A Great Dragon, or a Bandit for that matter, can hardly scratch a Banshee, let alone a main battle tank, without careful aim. Reality check, anyone?)<<<<<
—Sten (12:32:49/10-21-54)

>>>>(Too bad that on the high end, armor technology is outpacing armor-piercing technology. That state of affairs began nearly twenty years ago, when the new alloy-composite armor hit the field. Fortunately, the best stuff still costs plenty.)<<<<<
—Matador
(02:10:09/10-25-54)

>>>>>(Remember that the Dragon is a man-portable weapon, not a vehicle-mounted anti-armor weapon. These are nasty fraggers.)<<<<<
—Leaguer
(12:25:10/10-29-54)

>>>>>(Yeah, but the vehicle-mounted Bandit AGM doesn't even have the armor penetration of a Great Dragon. I guess being airborne, it needs to be lighter. . .)<<<<<
—Arnie Leech
(08:26:28/11-05-54)

BALLISTA MULTI-ROLE MISSILE LAUNCHER

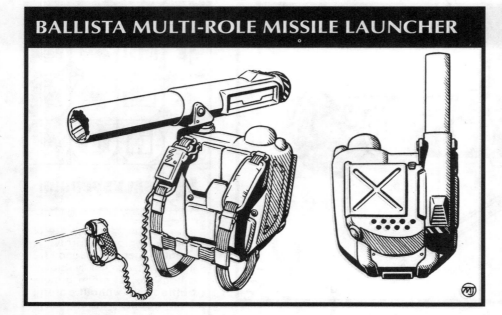

Manufactured by Saeder-Krupp's infamous Special Munitions branch, the sophisticated Ballista consists of a backpack mechanism that deploys a shoulder-firing missile tube. The Ballista missile can be used with the launcher inclined as an indirect-fire weapon, or as a direct-fire weapon balanced on the shoulder. The indirect-fire system revolves around microtronic compensators that align the tube at the proper angle regardless of the firer's position with respect to true vertical, and can fire Ballista Mk I or Mk II rounds. The direct-fire system operates similarly to other missile launchers and can fire Mk I, II, and III Ballista missiles.

Type	Conceal	Ammo	Mode	Damage	Weight	Availability	Cost	Street Index
Missile	—	4 (m)	SS	14D	6.5	18/30 days	10,500¥	4

*See Weapon Range Table, p. 87.

See following page for information on Ballista rounds. Each type of magazine contains 4 rounds and can be replaced in 10 seconds. The Ballista itself takes 30 seconds to remove or put on, and has no rear blast zone. The weapon comes with a Type I Laser Designator (see pp. 85-86) for use in direct-fire mode only.

SALESPERSON

>>>>>(This device is vastly overpriced and too sophisticated for the common merc. Stick with weapons that are internally smart and don't need outside guidance. They're not infallible, but you can fire 'em and forget 'em.)<<<<<
—Matador
(02:12:41/10-25-54)

>>>>>(It fits the "Future Trooper" concept, though: hardened battle armor, integrated comm and tactical data links, integral weapons, and so on. A laser-designator is only one of many targeting systems the Ballista can use; this weapon is modular and therefore easy to upgrade.)<<<<<
—Colonel Cobra
(14:03:20/11-02-54)

>>>>>(Picture this: a High-Spy sensor drone roams the battlefield using a multifaceted sensor suite with infrared, thermal and radar imaging, optical recognition, and so on to identify hostiles. When it finds one, it downloads the targeting data—range and angle of launch and descent—to a viable friendly. The Ballista takes the data link, adjusts itself, and fires. The soldier just approves the launch.)<<<<<
—Sten (20:11:29/11-05-54)

BALLISTA ROCKET & MISSILE ROUNDS

Custom-designed for the Saeder-Krupp Ballista launcher, Ballista rockets and missiles use a variety of warheads and targeting configurations. All types of rounds can be mixed and matched within a single magazine.

	Intelligence	Damage	Blast	Weight	Cost	Availability	Street Index
Mk I	0	14D	–7/meter	2.75	1,000¥	12/21 days	4
Mk II	5*	14D	–7/meter	2.75	2,000¥	18/28 days	4
Mk III	6	14 D	–7/meter	2.75	2,500¥	14/28 days	4

*See Reflected-Energy Designators, p. 85.

The Mk I is an armor-piercing, dumb rocket, used for direct or indirect fire. Apply grenade rules given on p. 96, **SRII.** The Mk II is an armor-piercing, laser-tracking missile used for direct and indirect fire. See Reflected-Energy Designators, p. 85 of this book. The Mk III is an armor-piercing, semi-smart missile used only for direct fire.

>>>>>(Continuing from comments on the Ballista launcher, why bother with a soldier? Why not just use field drones?)<<<<<
—Tony's Tiger
(20:41:09/11-08-54)

>>>>>(Eventually, they will. Plenty of people are investing meganuyen in hyper-expert and AI systems for combat vehicles. Some designers see flesh as a weak link; after all, you can't scare a computer.)<<<<<
—Colonel Cobra
(03:20:18/11-09-54)

>>>>>(We're a long way from developing an AI system capable of processing the same degree of data that the human mind can handle, despite what some corps might want you to think. Even the best parallel processors ain't savvy enough.)<<<<<
—Weird Wanda
(18:29:30/11-10-54)

>>>>>(You just keep thinking that, Wanda.)<<<<<
—Nightfire (20:04:15/11-11-54)

M-12 MAN-PORTABLE MORTAR

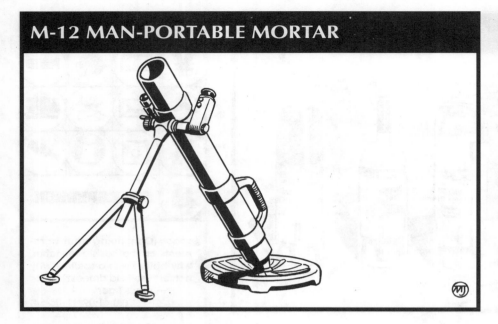

SALESPERSON

An extremely dependable weapon, the M-12 mortar is based on a battle-proven design. Its long barrel ends in a four-pronged base that digs into and anchors the weapon against the ground, and a swing-out, bipod brace props the weapon at a firing angle. The weapon's operator enters firing angles and environmental conditions manually into the controls of the barrel-mounted sight. In addition to sighting and firing the weapon himself, the operator can fire based on data from a spotter. The M-12 can fire "dumb" rounds or sophisticated, laser-tracking ammo.

Type	Conceal	Ammo	Mode	Damage	Weight	Availability	Cost	Street Index
Mortar	—	1	SS	Special	30	12/14 days	3,000¥	2

See rules for smoke and white phosphorous mortars, pp. 85-86 of this book. For information on the M-12's special mortar rounds, see the following page. The mortar takes 3 minutes, or 36 turns, to set up and 18 turns to break down. It fires up to 2 rounds per Combat Turn, regardless of the number of Actions the firer has available.

>>>>>(Mortars. I keep thinking of the sysop's message up front, that a lot of the stuff in these files would interest shadowrunners. A mortar? A fraggin' mortar? Cut me loose!)<<<<<
—Singapore Sami
(21:05:48/10-25-54)

>>>>>(A mortar might not be useful? I beg to differ. Maybe it's not part of a runner's day-to-day pack o' goodies, but it can come in handy. I orchestrated a run against a corp compound outside Los Angeles about two years ago, and my team peppered the area with smoke rounds as we went in. Filled the place up good. We used thermal sighting, which the corp boys didn't have. Going out, we also dropped a couple of HE rounds into the motor pool to discourage pursuit. Worked well.)<<<<<
—Kingslayer
(20:28:36/10-29-54)

>>>>>(Kingslayer has a good point. A runner needs to look at more than the weapons he has on hand; to make a run work, construct a sound plan and then get the gear to make that plan work. Assuming any runner plans realistically, of course.)<<<<<
—Hatchetman
(13:07:19/11-05-54)

MORTAR ROUNDS

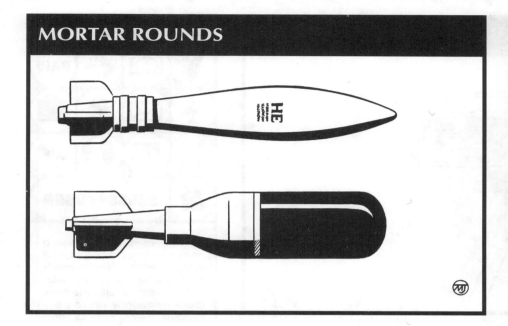

The M-12 Mortar takes all the types of rounds listed below. All rounds are drop-fired down the mortar barrel, their self-contained motors ignited by a pin at the barrel's bottom. All are fin-stabilized in flight, and arm only after they have cleared the barrel.

	Damage	Blast	Weight	Cost	Availability	Street Index
High Explosive	18D	−1/ .5m	4.0	200¥	18/14 days	3
Anti-Personnel*	18D	−1/ 1m	4.0	250¥	18/14 days	3
Smoke**	—	—	3.5	175¥	14 days	2
White Phosphorus†	15S/12L	−1/ 1m	4.0	350¥	18/14 days	3
Anti-Vehicle††	16D	−1/ 4m	4.0	1,200¥	21 days	4

*Use the **Flechette** rules, p. 93, **SRII.**
**See p. 85 of this book.
†See p. 86 of this book.
††This armor-piercing round's laser-tracking seeker requires a laser-marked target (see **Target Designators**, p. 85 of the **Rules** section).

>>>>>(White phosphorus? I've got scars from that drek. I was working in Africa when a light plane buzzed our camp. Fraggin' plane carried a brace of rockets that the pilot dropped on us like bombs. They burst and spread phosphorus over the whole area.
A year later, I found the pilot and skinned him like he'd done to me.)<<<<<
—Night Hunter
(13:10:23/10-24-54)

>>>>>(Technically, white phosphorus is a chemical weapon and should fall under appropriate international guidelines. Though it rarely kills, it inflicts at least third-degree burns even through normal clothing. Using white phosphorus saddles your opponent with quite a problem—he has to care for many more wounded. It's so much easier to bury the dead.)<<<<<
—Colonel Cobra
(05:20:14/11-05-54)

>>>>>(A real solider; always the humane reaction.)<<<<<
—Tecker (19:38:45/11-06-54)

>>>>>(It's real warfare, Tecker. If you fight, you fight to win. Anything less is inhumane.)<<<<<
—Matador
(04:20:31/11-09-54)

SENTRY WEAPONS

The long-awaited Ares Arms Sentry™ weapons have finally arrived! The Sentry™ platform's unique modular system allows a merc or sec-force to customize it to suit specific needs. A fully-functioning "smart" system, a Sentry™ can recognize, track, and engage pre-set, situation-determined, or random targets within its zone of control. Its multi-aspect sensors cover the entire electromagnetic spectrum, allowing it to engage any target it can sense for effective, deadly control.

Intelligence	Concealability	Weight	Cost	Availability	Street Index
6†	—	4.0*	22,000¥††	12/21 days	4

*Plus weight of weapon, accessories, and ammunition.
†Each new sensor purchased adds +1 to the weapon's Intelligence Rating.
††Standard weapon costs 22,000¥, plus 10 percent of purchase price for customization. Purchase ammo and recoil compensation per standard rules. Additional low-light, pulsed radar, ultrasound, and audio sensors with integration software/hardware cost 2,000¥ each. Improved targeting capability allows the gun barrel to incline 20° and decline 10° at a cost of 3,000¥.

All Sentry™ weapons include integrated thermographic and pulse-radar sensors. All have a base Initiative of 15 + 1D6, which can be raised to 20 + 2D6 at a cost of 10,000¥ or to 25 + 2D6 at a cost of 20,000¥. Every Sentry™ has the equivalent of Firearms Skill 5, increased by +1 at a cost of 5,000¥ and by +1 for every additional integrated sensor purchased. The Sentry™ system takes 5 minutes to assemble or take apart, and is designed around a tripod that holds a motorized weapon mount with 360-degree rotation. The tripod provides 6 points of Recoil Compensation. The weapon mount holds any weapon from a submachine gun to a light machine gun, including new HVAR and HV/LMG weapons. Ammunition is belt-fed from a protected store that holds up to 2,000 rounds. For purposes of attacks against the system, the Sentry™ has a Barrier Rating of 12. For rules on Sentry™ gun operation, see **Rules**, p. 83.

Counts as Hardpoint

>>>>>(I've run into these a couple of times during regular merc work and "shadowrun"-style ops. Perimeter and "hazardous area" security use them more frequently these days because they're easy to transport and set up. Also damn effective.)<<<<<
—Matador
(04:20:45/11-05-54)

>>>>>(Ares is building a whole industry around these bastards. Future options include optical recognition technology (you get shot if you look wrong), active sensor interrogation (you get shot if you don't have the right coded badge), and mobile-platform integration.)<<<<<
—Conqueror Wyrm
(20:10:32/11-08-54)

>>>>>(Mobile platform integration??)<<<<<
—Weasel (05:24:23/11-09-54)

>>>>>(Already mentioned in the MAW entry. Main battle tanks and others have APZs—anti-personnel zones—covered by automated, anti-infantry weapons mounted on the vehicle. Most tanks use Sentry guns or their ilk, or flechette/HE directional charges for close targets.)<<<<<
—Colonel Cobra
(06:20:19/11-09-54)

ARMTECH MGL-12

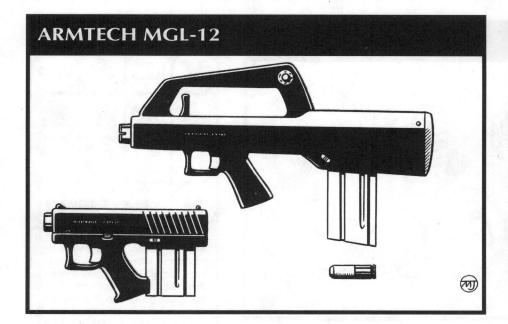

Ever felt bothered by the limited ammo your under-barrel grenade launcher carries? The ArmTech MGL-12 multi-grenade launcher ends all your worries. A simple bull-pup weapon, the MGL-12 can load a clip of twelve standard mini-grenades. Accurate to a range of 300 meters, the MGL-12 lets you deliver all the blast you need! Also available in a Mini-6, pistol-style version!

Type	Conceal	Ammo	Mode	Damage	Weight	Availability	Cost	Street Index
Grenade12	3	12 (c)	SA	Variable *	5.0	6/36	2,200¥	3
Grenade 6	6	6 (c)	SA	Variable*	2.5	6/36	1,600¥	3

*Use standard grenade rules, p. 96, **SRII**.

Recoil modifier is +2. Recoil compensation only applies to gyro-mounts. The weapon accepts targeting and sighting accessories.

>>>>>(Ya know, nobody's said the most important thing about all this wiz gear. Don't use it unless you know how, 'kay? Dumbest thing I ever saw was a bulked-out street sam running down the street with an MGL-12, trying to hit a fast-retreating Hughes Stallion. Thought I was watching one of those *Armed to the Teeth* sims.)<<<<<
　　—Airman Al
　　　　(04:20:29/11-06-54)

>>>>>(Hey! *I HIT THE FRAGGIN' THING!* So shut the frag up before I make you eat my fist!)<<<<<
　　—Slugg (09:20:14/11-07-54)

>>>>>(Bad news, Slugg-o-my-heart: *YOU MISSED!* You tagged the top of a tree, which blew up real nicely. I, however, piloting the aforementioned Stallion, made my escape. Guess you were too busy dodging bits of burning tree to notice. . .)<<<<<
　　—Airman Al
　　　　(20:15:48/11-09-54)

>>>>>(*YOU ARE MEAT! PASTY CAKES! DREK ON MY SHOE! SCUM IN THE BOTTOM OF THE BUCKET! FLESH BITS! WYRM FOOD! DEAD DEAD DEAD!* (I'm gonna kill ya and then I'm gonna eat ya!))<<<<<
　　—Slugg (10:14:19/11-10-54)

GRENADES

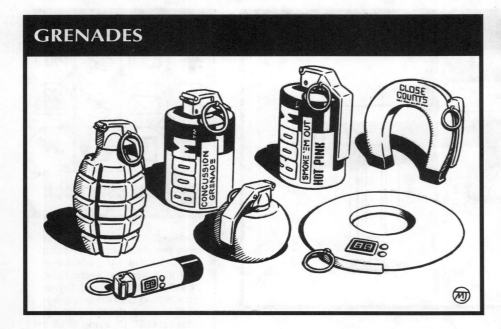

Grenades! Grenades! Grenades! One-stop shopping for all your grenade needs! Mix and match all shapes and sizes. Designer colors available.

Grenade Type	Conceal	Damage	Weight	Availability	Cost/Street Index
Offensive (HE* or AP)**	6	10S (–1/ meter)	.25	4 days	30¥/2
IPE Offensive (HE* or AP)**	6	15S (–1/meter)	.25	5/4 days	50¥/2
Defensive (HE* or AP)**	6	10S (–1/ .5 meter)	.25	4 days	30¥/2
IPE Defensive (HE* or AP)**	6	15S (–1/ .5 meter)	.25	5/4 days	50¥/2
Concussion	6	12M (Stun) (–1/ meter)	.25	5/4 days	30¥/2
IPE Concussion	6	16M (Stun) (–1/ meter)	.25	5/4 days	70¥/2
White Phosphorus***	6	14M/10L (–1/meter)	.25	6/5 days	120¥/3
Smoke†	6	—	.25	3/24 hrs	30¥/2
Smoke (IR)†	6	—	.25	4/48 hrs	40¥/2
Flash††	6	Special	.25	4/48 hrs	40¥/1
Mini-grenade	8	by grenade	.1	+2/by grenade	x2/+1

*HE: high-explosive. Standard grenade rules apply (p. 96, **SRII**).
AP: anti-personnel with high fragmentation. Standard grenade rules apply; determine damage according to flechette rules (p. 93, **SRII).
***See **Rules**, p. 86 of this book.
† See **Rules**, p. 85 of this book.
†† See p. 44, **Street Samurai Catalog**.

>>>>>(People vastly overestimate the effects of grenades. One old US Army study stated that an open-field grenade detonating within a few meters of a soldier had only an 80 percent chance of disabling him for a day. Of course, if you dive on the fraggin' thing like they keep doing in the sims, I'm sure the injuries get nastier.)<<<<<
—Tiny Terror
(21:38:49/11-05-54)

>>>>>(Don't believe everything you read. I don't trust any military study. Chip-truth, grenades make excellent herding weapons. Toss 'em in the right place and the enemy moves away from that location. Also, if your throwing arm or launcher is accurate, a grenade in the lap does a lot more damage than one that goes off "within a few meters.")<<<<<
—Hatchetman
(08:20:14/11-06-54)

>>>>>(Always remember to throw it after you arm it. Trust me.)<<<<<
—One-Handed Willy
(02:08:20/11-08-54)

ARES MP LASER III

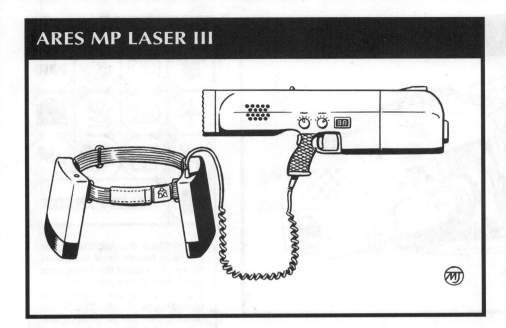

SALESPERSON

Ares Arms strikes again! Four years after introducing their revolutionary MP Laser, Ares has trimmed the price by an astounding 2,000 percent and begun mass production. An ideal weapon for the sophisticated mercenary or security force, the MP-Laser III is a self-contained, single-carrier system designed for instant reaction to and containment of serious threats. Hip-mounted, peak-discharge battery packs, designed for rapid exchange, can be recharged for future use.

Type	Conceal	Ammo	Mode	Damage	Weight	Availability	Cost	Street Index
Sniper	—	20	SA	15M	25	24/21 days	120,000¥	3

To determine range, consult the Weapon Range Table (see **Rules**, p. 87) and decrease the weapon's Power Level by −2 for each range beyond Short (Medium −2, Long −4, Extreme −6). Ballistic Armor has no effect; reduce Impact Armor by half, rounded down. The laser does not pierce armor, and suffers the standard −1 Damage reduction when used against vehicles. Smoke reduces the laser's Power Level by −1 for every 2 meters of smoke the beam passes through. Recoil modifiers do not apply.

>>>>>(*NOOOOOOOOOOO!* This has got to be bulldrek! Nothing drops in cost by *2,000 percent* in four years! Why are they marketing this jetwash? Why not just distribute assault rifles in grade school?!)<<<<<
—The Neon Samurai
(03:20:19/11-10-54)

>>>>>(I remember you had a problem with the original MP Laser in a posting some time ago. The MP Laser III is a lot less nasty than an assault cannon by a long shot, but it's still way too expensive for most to buy one. Why the tantrum, Neon?)<<<<<
—Findler-Man
(20:17:27/11-12-54)

>>>>>(Perhaps I can shed some light on this. For years, the Neon Samurai has spread slander against Ares Arms, claiming that the company killed a certain Doctor Elliot Mills-Fargo after he created the key patents for the MP Laser. This claim is untrue. Stephen Mills-Fargo, aka "The Neon Samurai," killed his own father after a drunken argument.)<<<<<
—Nightfire
(04:10:20/11-13-54)

ARES FIRELANCE™ VEHICLE LASER

SALESPERSON

Watch the next level of Ares MP Laser technology in action! Ares Arms has created the first viable laser system for small and medium-sized vehicles. The turret-mounted FireLance™ system offers anti-armor capability against lightly armored vehicles and low-flying aircraft. Its high recharge rate allows it to hit multiple targets with ease, and its focusing and emission system has an extraordinarily high mean time between failure. Top-notch firepower with a minimum of field service—buy an Ares laser and you can't go wrong!

Type	Conceal	Ammo	Mode	Damage	Weight	Availability	Cost	Street Index
Assault	—	40	SA	15S	48	Unknown	300,000¥	Unknown

To determine range, consult the Weapon Range Table (see **Rules**, p. 87). Decrease the weapon's Power Level by −2 for each range beyond Short (Medium −2, Long −4, Extreme −6). Ballistic Armor has no effect; reduce Impact Armor by half, rounding down. The armor-piercing beam suffers the standard −1 Damage Level reduction when used against vehicles. Smoke reduces the Power Level by −1 for every 4 meters of smoke the beam passes through. Recoil modifiers do not apply.

>>>>>(Nice try, Nightfire, you pathetic facsimile of a human being. Ares killed my father and *you know it*. I've been collecting the proof for years: I've almost got it all. You'll be among the first to twist in the wind. Watch your back, chummer; that freight-train behind you is me!)<<<<<
    —The Neon Samurai
        (10:21:40/11-14-54)

>>>>>(If you've got proof, go public with it. If you start a one-man war against Ares, you'll lose. I'm no corp-kisser, but I have a good grasp of reality. You are a single samurai; they are a trillion-nuyen, multinational megacorp. Don't take them on, Neon—I already have too many friends in cemeteries.)<<<<<
    —Hatchetman
        (08:20:10/11-15-54)

>>>>>(Neon Samurai can rave all he wants. Ares has proof he killed his father. Just before the Neon Samurai slammed his father's head through a plate-glass door, Dr. Mills-Fargo managed to press the house's PANICBUTTON™ and trigger Knight Errant's internal surveillance systems. We have him committing murder on trideo. If anyone wants a copy, e-mail me at NA/UCAS/MW/ARES-DET/42012093:NIGHTFIRE.DROP. The key portion is 30 Mps.)<<<<<
    —Nightfire
        (21:29:32/11-15-54)

AMMUNITION

The American Ammo Co. proudly announces improvements to its current explosive and tracer ammunition products. Now, the EXAmmo line provides more explosion and fragmentation than ever before, at a minimal cost increase. The ViewFlight line of tracer ammunition has also been updated to provide an even more accurate ballistic path and brighter burn! American Ammo; for all your ammo needs!

	Concealability	Damage	Weight	Availability	Cost	Street Index
EX Explosive	8	See below	.75	6/72 hrs	100¥	1.5
Tracer	8	See below	.5	3/24 hrs	75¥	1

EX explosive rounds add +2 to the Power of the weapon, but use all other standard rules. Tracer rounds can be used only in full-auto weapons, and are loaded every third round in the clip. Non-smartgun users receive an additional −1 target number modifier at ranges beyond Short, cumulative with every third round fired (−1 after first three, −2 after six, and so on). When calculating burst damage for three-round, multiple-round, or short-round bursts, do not add a bonus to the Power for the tracer round, but do increase the Damage Level appropriately. For example, a sub-machinegun using a 5M round and firing 10 rounds would have a Damage Code of 12D, normally 15D.

>>>>>(It's a common misconception that "exploding" rounds are like micro-grenades. Not true. Yes, there's a detonation, but the load is so minor it's really like an impressive fragmentation. Also, the rounds tend to detonate early, especially when punching through body armor of any weight. So no, you don't shoot somebody and then get to watch him blow up.)<<<<<
— Teague
(12:10:13/8-22-94)

>>>>>(I've heard that Ares or someone is working on an explosive compound that detonates on contact with moisture. It's like a plastic explosive, so it blows up good when it hits, say, a body. That will let you shoot somebody and watch them blow up.)<<<<<
— Gabe (21:51:52/8-22-94)

>>>>>(Geez! What are you, twelve years old or something? Think about what you just said. Moisture? That's got to be one of the dumbest things I've ever heard. Grow up. Get a life. Leave us alone.)<<<<<
— Monster Eater
(08:20:17/8-23-94)

CAMOUFLAGE CLOTHING

SALESPERSON

No field operation is complete without the proper clothing! Patterson Fabrics Camo-Spec™ clothing uses computer-designed environmental facsimile patterning for maximum concealment. Available in a wide variety of patterns and weights, Patterson Fabrics is the choice for you!

Available patterns include Desert, Snow, Woodland, Urban, and Winter Woodland. All garments have reversible day/night patterns.

	Ballistic	Impact	Availability	Cost	Street Index
Full Suit	3	1	4/36 hrs	800¥	1
Jacket	5	3	5/36 hrs	1,200¥	1

For the effects of camo clothing on Perception Tests, see **Rules,** p. 77.

>>>>>(Most shadowrunners don't think about clothing, though mercs live and die by it. Amazing how many wild-card, runner-wannabes try to sneak around in their Day-Glo Mohawk hairdos and phosphorescent tattoos.)<<<<<
—Hatchetman
(03:20:11/11-08-54)

>>>>>(Maybe they're intentionally unprepared. You know, "Zen and the Art of Shadowrunning?" Let the flow guide you. Ride the river, don't fight it. Be the wind.)<<<<<
—Whistle
(08:28:29/11-09-54)

>>>>>(Be real, chummer. Sure, you need some spontaneity, but if you know the course of the river ahead of time you'll be prepared to shift your weight to avoid the rocks. Know the course, and only wing it when you have to.)<<<<<
—Stick (17:29:41/11-11-54)

>>>>>(Remind me not to work on any missions with either of you two wonk-heads. Jeez.)<<<<<
—Raider X
(18:56:22/11-12-54)

GEL-PACK ARMOR

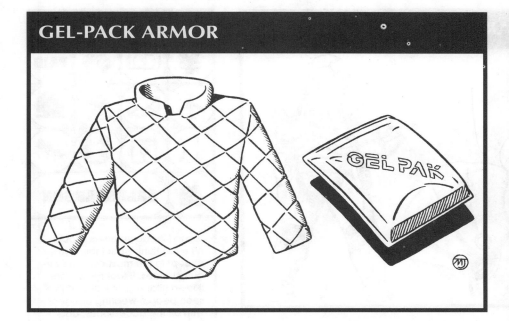

SALESPERSON

When you need something tougher than soft-cloth ballistic armor, step up to real protection. Kelmar Tech's patented gel-pack technology provides hardened protection against penetration along with maximum comfort and flexibility. Kelmar gel-packs remain liquid and flexible until the shock wave of a projectile impact solidifies the gel into an impenetrable barrier. As the kinetic energy dissipates, the gel liquefies, ready to absorb the next impact. Kelmar's military-spec combat armor is the best of the best!

Mil-spec gel packs can be added to any available armor. With the addition of gel-packs, treat armor as Hardened at its normal Ballistic and Impact ratings. If applicable, reduce Concealability by half (rounded down). The gel-packs increase all armor's weight by 25 percent, multiply its cost by 5, double its Street Index and Availability target number, and quadruple the time required to get it.

If a weapon's Power, before burst or autofire modifications, does not exceed the modified armor's rating, the round does not penetrate and does no damage. If a weapon's Power exceeds the armor's rating, reduce the rating per standard **Shadowrun** rules. Penetration reduces the armor's rating by 1 per penetration.

>>>>>(I used this gel drek once working in the south of France. We're geared for a little night action, so I'm strapped into a set of mil-spec light security armor and running a full electronics suite, interlinked with all my team members, exchanging data at the speed of light. We penetrate the complex and BOOM! my happy feet trigger a Sentry gun (sorry I ain't gonna type in that fraggin' (TM)!) sporting an HV/LMG. The burst knocks me back a couple of meters and leaves me staring at stars. Am I alive? Yup. Do I hurt? Oh, yeah. Can I move? Nooooo. Know why? The gel doesn't liquefy. It stays hard and leaves me stiff as a plank. The tech-heads told me it was a "multiple shock-wave resonance effect." One in a million, they said. Never happen again, they said. I won't play those odds.)<<<<<
    —Night Fighter
        (08:23:14/11-10-54)

>>>>>(I've found that mil-spec versions of most conventional armor is pointless against ballistics. It doesn't stop a round all that much better than soft-cloth armor, which is a misnomer: after all, plates are standard in soft body armor. Against blades, though, mil-spec comes in handy—assuming a troll doesn't take a stab at you.)<<<<<
    —Tuna Boy
        (10:20:11/11-13-54)

MILITARY GRADE ARMOR

SALESPERSON

The military traditionally kept the best for themselves. Now, Esprit Industries of France brings you mil-spec quality on the open market! Esprit's new line of military-grade combat armor offers full protection, hard and soft-armor integration, energy dispersal, thermal dampening options, intrasuit wiring conduits, surface antenna matrices, the works. Available in standard or custom camouflage patterns, these suits are a must for the serious fighter.

	Ballistic	Impact	Weight	Availability	Cost/Street Index
Light Military Armor	10	7	12 + Body	18/1 mth	25,000¥/3
Medium Military Armor	12	8	14 + Body	24/1 mth	45,000¥/3
Heavy Military Armor	14	9	16 + Body	28/1.5 mths	70,000¥/3
Heavy Military Helmet	+2	+3	3.0	24/1 mth	2,500¥/3

Treat military-grade armor as Hardened. Suits are designed to integrate combat electronics, including the BattleTac™ system. Military-grade armor reduces the wearer's Combat Pool by 1 for every 2 points of Ballistic Armor Rating above the character's Quickness Rating.

>>>>>(Shadowrunners shouldn't even think about this stuff except in the most extreme circumstances. It looks like what it is—military-grade armor. I've seen people wearing this gear with all the accessories, and they don't look human. Makes me shake to think about it.)<<<<<
—Rapid Fire
(08:21:28/11-09-54)

>>>>>(I heard Fuchi's working on a fully-powered version of this kind of armor: strength amplification, jump-pack system, integrated weapons, the works. Anybody else heard anything?)<<<<<
—Shade
(20:21:28/11-13-54)

>>>>>(Just rumors, but I heard it was Ares, not Fuchi.)<<<<<
—Hyper-Volt
(17:25:40/11-24-54)

>>>>>(Fuchi? That'll be the day.)<<<<<
—Nightfire
(08:27:35/11-25-54)

COUGAR FINE BLADE KNIFE

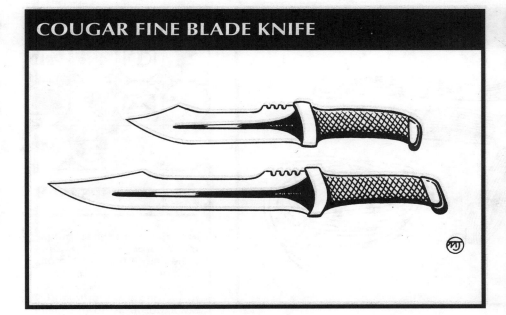

SALESPERSON

Ideal for the in-the-field mercenary or the more urban oriented soldier of fortune, the Cougar Fineblade uses state-of-the-art molecular bonding and edging technology to create an incomperable blade. Its double-bladed, with a special wire-cutting notch, and hardened grip and pommel, makes the Cougar Fineblade the perfect combat companion. Available in standard and long-blade versions, both using Cougar's patented technology.

	Concealability	Reach	Damage	Weight	Availability	Cost	Street Index
Short Blade	8	—	(STR)M	.5	5/72 hrs	800¥	3
Long Blade	5	—	(STR + 1)M	.75	8/72 hrs	1,500¥	3

The Fineblade knife has no special properties.

>>>>>(This is an interesting weapon option that offers much the same effect as Dikoting™ at a greatly reduced price. Ironically, at a weapons show in Cairo last year I watched a salesman show this weapon to an interested young lady, in the process severing two fingers. Quite a demonstration.)<<<<<
—Tyrus (8-15-94/3:20:14)

>>>>>(Dikote™ is more effective, especially because it has anti-armor capability. Fletcher, a friend of mine with an almost unnatural affection for archery, uses Dikote™ arrowheads almost exclusively— to great effect. I've also seen Dikote™-coated crossbow bolts blow straight through an armored passenger car and come out the other side pretty bloody.)<<<<<
—Dennis 'D'
(13:11:18/8-21-94)

>>>>>(Since this conversation seems to have digressed to discussing Dikote™, I'll offer an evil thought. . . Has anyone considered or experimented with Dikoting flechettes? Just wondering.)<<<<<
—Weasel Boy
(21:10:41/08-21-94)

CLIMBING GEAR

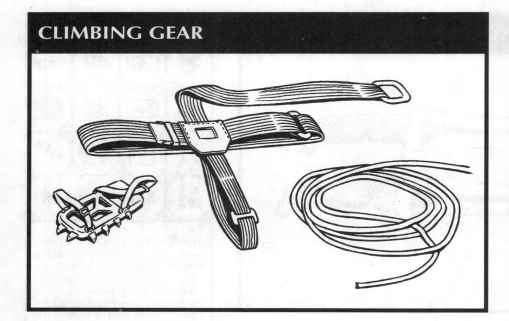

Sometimes, getting in is half the battle; Duraflex's full line of climbing accessories tips the battle in your favor! Built for the soldier on the move, all Duraflex accessories are compact, efficient, and reliable. Count on Duraflex!

	Weight	Availability	Cost	Street Index
Ascent/Descent Harness	.25	Always	75¥	1
Ascent/Descent Kit*	2.0	Always	250¥	1
Rappelling Gloves	—	Always	70¥	1
Rope (50m)	1.0	Always	125¥	1

*Ascent/Descent kit includes descenders, ascenders, carabiners, crampons, and so on as appropriate.

All climbing ropes and harnesses hold up to 2,000 kgs. Harness is quick-release. For climbing rules, see pp. 75-76.

>>>>>(One of my best career moves was to learn mountaineering. I feel much more confident, so I can ascend, descend, and traverse much faster and more efficiently. My exposure is down significantly, and I am a much happier troll.)<<<<<
—Able (04:28:28/11-05-54)

>>>>>(WOW! Sorry, I just flashed on walking down the street and seeing a troll rappelling down a skyscraper toward me. One question that only just occurred to me: how easily available is troll- and ork-sized gear? I see so-called "normal" stuff everyday, but what about "Real Big Man" stuff?)<<<<<
—Lord Fly
(21:28:15/11-08-54)

>>>>>(Some things are more common than others. For example, I can simply buy some climbing gear at a greater tensile strength than anything small folk would buy for themselves. In general, though, ork-sized stuff costs 50 percent more and troll-sized stuff doubles in price. Bulldrek like that keeps my people in the slums.)<<<<<
—Able (05:10:13/11-10-54)

SMARTLINK LEVEL II

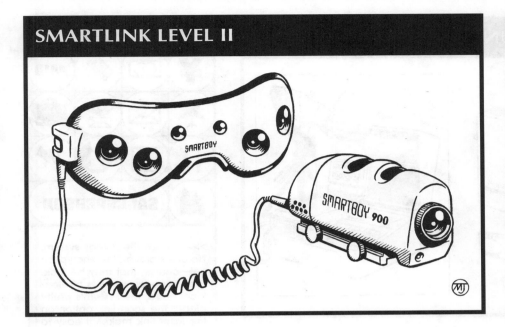

Available for the first time, the new Smartlink Level II represents a significant improvement over existing smartgun technology. Better command processing, faster signal referencing, cleaner cross-vendor integration, and formal adherence to the new ADVAT.328 protocol standards make your weapon linkage faster and better than ever! Smartlink Level II components are fully compatible with Level I Smartlink systems!

	Mount	Conceal	Weight	Availability	Cost	Street Index
External	Top/under	–2	.75	6/48 hrs	800¥	2
Internal	—	—	.25	Weapon	+250%	Weapon
Smartgoggles	—	0	.1	4/36 hrs	3,500¥	2

	Essence Cost	Availability	Cost	Street Index
Smartlink	.5	6/48 hrs	3,200¥	2

For rules regarding Smartlink Level II technology, see p. 84-85. To gain Level II advantages, both the smartlink and the smartgun must be Level II.

>>>>>(Truthfully, I wonder if the upgrade is worth the price. Most of the improvements really only matter to tech-heads. The weapon feels more alert (weird sensation), and the range finder linkage becomes handy at longer ranges, but I just don't know.)<<<<<
—Fitzburg
(03:29:16/11-12-54)

>>>>>(Fitz, old boy, for some of us that uncertainty makes the package.)<<<<<
—Grouper
(20:18:16/11-13-54)

>>>>>(The specs don't say anything about it, but I just got a Smartlink Level II and it interfaces with my vehicle control rig. I get full status and targeting info off any "smart" vehicle weapon when I'm rigging, in addition to the standard basic data overlays. I'm definitely more accurate with smartlinked weapons now. I found all this out because I needed to swap out an LMG that had fouled. The only one we had was already "smart," and I didn't have time to take out the brains.)<<<<<
—Georgi
(23:29:41/11-15-54)

>>>>>(Hey! Mine doesn't do that. . .)<<<<<
—Radar Lover
(14:31:23/11-17-54)

TACTICAL COMMUNICATION SYSTEM

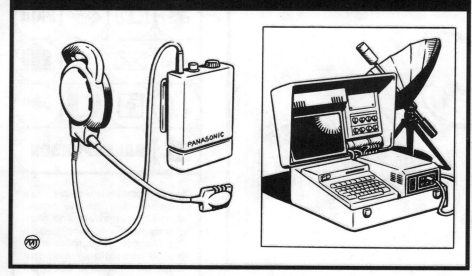

Keep in touch with the rest of your team with the new Phillips Tacticom system! Phillips brings its combat-proven electronics to battlefield communications with six levels of signal encryption and the capability to load custom encryption algorithms. Heavily protected both inside and out, the master unit accepts signals from conventional land-lines, satellite uplinks, dedicated laser-links, microwave relay, and any other telecommunications signal source. An outstanding system at an outstanding price!

Index	Concealability	Rating	Weight	Availability	Cost	S t r e
Master Unit	—	14	75	24/21 days	60,000¥	3
Portable Master Unit	—	14	20	18/14 days	120,000¥	2
Personal Comm Unit	8	14	.5	12/14 days	18,500¥	2
Microwave Link	3	—	1.0	18/21 days	4,800¥	2
Laser Link	4	—	1.0	14/21 days	2,700¥	2
Satellite Uplink	—	—	2.0	12/21 days	7,500¥	2

For more information on the uses of the system, see p. 86.

SALESPERSON

>>>>>(I like the Phillips system. No one's broken the encryption yet—course, that may be luck. Even in zones with lots of electrical noise, the system's pretty clean. The scan-link option on the laser link makes it easy to set one up and hit the receptor—get the bearing right, and the system does the work. Slick.)<<<<<
—Matador
(03:51:30/11-15-54)

>>>>>(I prefer to work off a laser or tight-beam satellite system. (Frag, I've even lofted a hover-drone with a microwave link system. My boys knew where it was and could tap it for direct-link communication. Of course, we were all on-line with BattleTac™ hardware. After all, we're the best!)<<<<<
—Winter Rat
(20:16:35/11-16-54)

>>>>>(Thanks Rat— I'll remember that next time we tangle.)<<<<<
—Matador
(11:28:06/11-19-54)

>>>>>(Thailand again. Betcha.)<<<<<
—Winter Rat
(20:27:L13/11-21-54)

BATTLETAC™ INTEGRATION SYSTEM

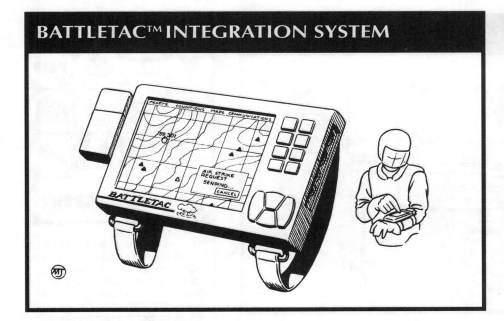

SALESPERSON

Sony makes a splash in battlefield tactical management with the BattleTac™ system! In the field, knowledge is power—the BattleTac™ system gives that power to the commanders and to the soldier on the line. Unit positions, assets, conditions, situations—you name it and BattleTac™ has it!

The BattleTac™ system integrates tactical telecommunications and data transfer. Each soldier equipped with a BattleTac™ unit is linked with allied BattleTac™ users in an open communications and data exchange network. Sony Corp's BattleTac™ gives you the key to victory!

Using BattleTac™ requires Military Science skill, or preferably the Small Unit Tactics Specialization of that skill, and the Special Skill BattleTac™ (acquired as per a General Skill (page 190, **SRII**, after character generation). See also page 84 for more information. Users receive an additional –2 modifier to all relevant target numbers when the network is active.

77

>>>>>(Sorry, chummers. This drek means the "Future Trooper" is now. See, vehicles can also use BattleTac™. Let's say Dog Soldier Sylvia sees an enemy unit approaching her hideaway. She feeds that data into the network, and seconds later a trio of Stonewall MBTs sitting silently in a field kilometers away start dropping death on the enemy unit. Imagine this kind of hook-up with artillery, air-to-ground weapons, homing mortar rounds, and so on. The modern battlefield is data, people. Believe it, or die.)<<<<<
—Matador
(11:34:29/11-19-54)

>>>>>(We deckers have said that for years.)<<<<<
—Dead Deckers Society
(20:10:15/11-20-54)

>>>>>(Very funny. Fortunately, BattleTac™ systems and those like it are restricted to elite corporate or private units. You won't see a regular Aztlan trooper sporting BattleTac™ or anything like it.)<<<<<
—Cornwall
(03:27:51/11-22-54)

>>>>>(Give them time. Every year, prices and size drop by 10 percent. Welcome to progress.)<<<<<
—I in the Sky
(18:46:30/11-24-54)

TARGET DESIGNATORS

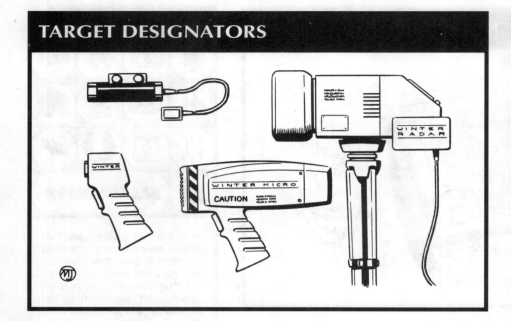

Light up that enemy! Winter Systems offers top-of-the-line target designators. Choose the target of allied fire from the safety of your bunker, trench, or hideaway with the front-runner in military electronics. From IR lasers to microwave pulse systems, Winter Systems designators are the most accurate and reliable model on the market. When precision counts, count on Winter!

Type	Conceal	Range	Weight	Availability	Cost	Street Index
Low-power laser sight	−1	500m	.25	6/36 hrs	500¥	.9
High-power laser sight	−1	1,500m	.25	8/48 hrs	1,400¥	1
Laser designator	−2	5,000m	.5	12/14 days	3,700¥	2
Microwave designator	—	8,000 m	4.5	24/1 mth	12,500¥	2
Radar designator	—	10,000 m+	25	24/3 mths	48,000¥	2

For rules on using target designators, see p. 85.

>>>>>(I've had a lot of success outfitting forward observers with various designators. They spot a target, light it up, and then the light artillery grunts in the backfield send up a handful of target tracking rounds. They grab some air, look down, and well-what-do-you-know, there are the targets shining brightly. Down they come. Boom goes the target. Gotta love it.)<<<<<
—Night Fighter (08:22:30/11-19-54)

>>>>>(Most designators can be compromised, so don't bet the farm on them or you just might end up buying that particular real estate. Smoke blocks lasers. Chaff—reflective particles blown into the air—nails microwave and radar. So do competing beams of microwave or radar energy. Never assume something will work; always plan alternatives.)<<<<<
—Matador (05:08:30/11-22—54)

>>>>>(Hey, Matty, do you teach merc for a living or something? Your tone is gettin' on my nerves, chummer. Scan me?)<<<<<
—Squirrel (13:38:50/11-24-54

>>>>>(You might say he wrote the book.)<<<<<
—Double Dirk (20:19:15/11-25-54)

GLOBAL POSITIONING SYSTEM

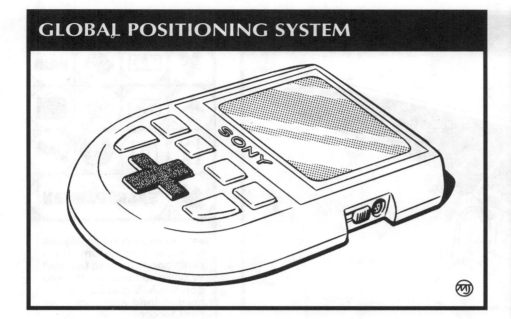

With the new Sony Nav-Dat™ global positioning system, you'll never get lost again! It instantly cross-references your location against all known navigational satellites and, in seconds, provides information on your location accurate within 2 meters. The system's super-accurate internal digital maps come datasoft jack-equipped, and cover several areas. The system also provides several standard coordinate systems and positioning algorithms. Plot, track, and plan your movements using the positions of the moon and sun: no bother, no hassle! Fully compatible with the Sony BattleTac™ system!

Concealability	Weight	Availability	Cost	Street Index
8	.5	6/48 hrs	700¥	1

>>>>>(Never get lost in Amazonia. Chummer, that place is so Awakened that any map made more than a month ago is out of date. I've never actually seen the land change, but I've been back to plenty of places I'd visited before and found them very, very different.)<<<<<
—Matador
(04:20:12/11-13-54)

>>>>>(I know for a fact that Amazonia purchased two Fuchi LandScan ground-imaging satellites about five years ago. Ares shot them into orbit about a year later. They pass over the whole country, re-imaging the entire nation once every three weeks. And they still use plenty of aircraft to monitor forest growth.)<<<<<
—I in the Sky
(07:02:16/11-14-54)

>>>>>(Amazonia's overgrowth problem is one of their dirty little secrets. Whatever they did to re-grow the rain forests seems to go on unchecked. I understand they've even considered limited, strategic deforestation in some areas, though you can imagine the political repercussions of that choice in the Green Nation.)<<<<<
—Mike Monitor
(10:57:32/11-15-54)

NIGHT GLIDER™

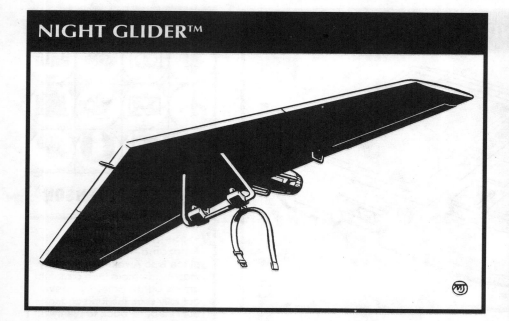

SALESPERSON

The Artemis Industries Nightglider™ brings the medium-weight glider to the cutting edge of infiltration operations. Easily deployable from two over-sized bags, the Nightglider™ runs on a compact, virtually silent, electric-driven turbofan engine. Low noise, radar-absorbing mesh skin, and a flexible and responsive airframe combine to make a vehicle perfect for midnight runs. The Nightglider™ can also carry a fully operational 400-kg load, making it ideal for full-gear tactical strikes. An optional remote operations package lets you leave it airborne nearby for a quick getaway!

Handling	Speed	B/A	Sig	APilot	Cost
3	15/60	1/0	12	1	45,000¥

Seating: 1 underslung
Access: N/A
Economy: 1 PF per km
Power: Elec/100
Cargo: 4 CFs
Weight: 200 kgs
Landing/Takeoff Profile: Effective VTOL
Additional Features: The glider takes 5 minutes to assemble and disassemble.

>>>>>(I've used the Nightglider on several occasions. It's a pretty good transport, but don't try anything fancy or it'll come apart. Avoid ground fire and hard landings at all costs.)<<<<<
—Matador
(04:29:17/11-10-54)

>>>>>(I also question the landing/takeoff information. Landing vertically is easy, because the stall-speed is so low you can pretty much coast in and land it, like a hang glider. Taking off is another story. You can take her up almost vertically by redlining the engine, but that sucks away about 25 percent of your battery power. It also kicks engine heat way up, which wrecks the bird's signature—but if you've got the watts to spare, go for it. You'll get off the ground fast.)<<<<<
—Desert Vet
(20:14:23/11-15-54)

>>>>>(I wish the airframe was a little tougher. It can take a firmpoint, and I usually bring up light cargo like ECM/ECCM gear and some sensors, but I still feel vulnerable.)<<<<<
—Trap Door Tex
(21:18:41/11-16-54)

GMC MPUV

SALESPERSON

The GMC multi-purpose utility vehicle (MPUV) is the world's most popular light combat vehicle, perfect for every use from light scout to personnel transport. Lightly armored against small-arms fire, the four-wheel drive MPUV can handle almost any situation.

Handling	Speed	B/A	Sig	APilot	Cost
5/3	40/120*	2/9	4	0	22,000¥

Seating: 2 front buckets + 1 rear bench   **Access:** 2 + 2 standard
Economy: 15 km per liter   **Fuel:** MultiF/100
Cargo: 10 CF
Additional Features: Accessories include a radio transceiver, white-light searchlight, roll bars, and roof pintle mount with access hatch. Some MPUVs come with a single hardpoint. Weapons not included.
*Off-road speed is 30/90.

>>>>>(Ah, the ubiquitous MPUV. You can even see street-legal versions in some areas. Trés chic, don't ya know.)<<<<<
—Hummer Hal
(08:29:37/11-28-54)

>>>>>(This entry is too vague about the vehicle's real capabilities. I've seen versions mounting anti-tank weapons, local-area sensor platforms, even light anti-aircraft missiles or autocannons. The biggest problem, in my opinion, is that its armor is too weak to stand up to real weapons and its relatively poor signature.)<<<<<
—Colonel Cobra
(21:02:21/11-30-54)

>>>>>(Sure, but trying to improve signature cripples the vehicle. The engine can't handle the extra load. I knew a merc unit that sensor-masked a bunch of MPUVs. Fraggin' things kept overheating. They could have installed extra coolant systems, but that gets expensive.)<<<<<
—Tiger Team
(20:54:28/12-02-54)

LAV-98 "DEVIL RAT" APC

SALESPERSON

The major transport of both the Confederated American States and California Free State, the Devil Rat armored personnel carrier (APC) is part of the arsenals of the world's major militaries and corporations. Able to deploy up to eight soldiers while providing fire support, the Devil Rat is the perfect choice for combat and combat-support missions.

Handling	Speed	B/A	Sig	APilot	Cost
5/3	25/75*	3/12	6	2	250,000¥

Seating: 3 crew + 3 benches

Access: 3 top hatches, 1 double-sized rear hatch

Economy: 2 km per liter

Cargo: 12 CF

Sensors: None

Fuel: MultiF/325 liters

ECM/ECCM: None

Additional Features: Amphibious capability, telecommunications system (Rating 0), EnviroSeal™, small remote turret. Weapons, sensors, and ECM/ECCM not included. Off-road speed is 15/45, 10/30 in water.

>>>>>(Devil Rat's a death trap if you ask me. I've seen too many of them light up after a hit near the ammo or fuel. The armor seems sufficient for its job, but ya gotta wonder when they go off like grenades all over the battlefield.)<<<<<
—Cougar Punch
(03:21:27/11-30-54)

>>>>>(Poor maintenance, Coug. Check those maintenance and tech people. Are they sealing all the conduits after servicing? Checking regularly for micro-leaks in the fuel lines, too small to notice but big enough for a fireball or spark to set off? Are the seals on the ammo feeds and bins solid or rotted? If someone's checking and you still got problems, you got a saboteur.)<<<<<
—Flying Wallenchek
(21:34:09/12-01-54)

>>>>>(I'll second that. We field Devil Rats regularly and have had no problems. Sure, they pop when an ATGM hits them, but that's no surprise.)<<<<<
—Winter Rat
(18:43:55/12-05-54)

LAV-103 "STRIKER" LIGHT TANK

SALESPERSON

Based on a reinforced version of the popular Devil Rat suspension and drive train, the LAV-103 "Striker" light tank has heavier armor and packs a heavier punch without loss of speed! Improvements to the engine and transmission enable this heavy fire-support vehicle to match the speeds of lighter tanks. Comes in amphibious and anti-air configurations, making the Striker a popular vehicle in many theaters of operation.

Handling	Speed	B/A	Sig	APilot	Cost
6/4	25/75*	5/15	6	2	480,000¥

Seating: 3 bucket seats

Economy: 1.5 km per liter
Cargo: 5 CF
Sensors: None
Additional Features: Comes with telecommunications system (Rating 0), and EnviroSeal™, and medium remote turret. Weapons not included.
*Off-road speed is 15/45.

Access: 2 front hatches,
1 turret hatch
Fuel: MultiF/600 liters
ECM/ECCM: None

>>>>>(The Striker configuration we use most often mounts a Victory rotary assault cannon. We've tried to construct the unit around the same class of heavy weapons so that they all use variants on the same ammo. It works pretty well, though obviously we'd like the heavier firepower of an actual autocannon on occasion.)<<<<<
     —Ultra-Drek
     (23:59:30/12-01-54)

>>>>>(Ultra, you are weird. I've never heard of such a thing on the scale you're talking. Maybe for small arms, but for cannon rounds?)<<<<<
     —Tuber
     (20:20:14/12-02-054)

>>>>>(Not really weird. I've worked with plenty of low-budget countries that bought their vehicles surplus. Want to hear about a logistical nightmare? Of the seven different kinds of light combat vehicles they fielded, none fired the same ammo. Yeeesh.)<<<<<
     —Merc Mania
     (18:28:41/12-030-54)

>>>>>(Seven different cannons in the same class?? That's stupid!!!)<<<<<
     —Weasel
          (04:21:40/12-06-54)

C-60 TITAN MEDIUM TRANSPORT

A common sight in corporate, military, and mercenary forces around the world, the C-260 is the perfect workhorse. With the right modifications, this transport can become a powerful air-to-ground weapons platform or a long-range sensor platform. An excellent all-purpose aircraft!

Handling	Speed	B/A	Sig	APilot	Cost
7	150/350	5/12	4	3	700,000¥

Seating: 2 crew (buckets) + 3 support (buckets)

Economy: .04
Max Range: 7,600 km
Cargo: 3,000 CF
Landing/Takeoff Profile: STOL
Sensors: None
Additional Features: Telecommunications system (Rating 0). Weapon mounts, sensors, and ECM/ECCM not included in standard configuration.

Access: 1 side hatch, rear ramp
Fuel: 180,000 liters
Combat Radius: 1,800 km
ECM/ECCM: None

>>>>>(This sucker flies like a fraggin' brick wall. If you're flying one of these and somebody shoots a marginally intelligent missile at you, or (god forbid) comes after you in an aircraft, you'd better hope you've got enough electronics to spook them. You sure as hell ain't gonna fly out of trouble.)<<<<<
—Wildcat
(13:56:41/12-03-54)

>>>>>(Heh. You've never seen one of our Titans, have you? Sensor suite to dream over: underwing AAMs, chaff and flare dispensers, the works. Costs money, but it's cheaper than losing the plane.)<<<<<
—Winter Rat
(04:20:53/12-05-54)

>>>>>(Or the pilot.)<<<<<
—Marx
(20:29:35/12-06-54)

>>>>>(Thanks for the thought!)<<<<<
—Wildcat
(14:08:01/12-07-54)

AERODESIGN CONDOR II LD SD-41

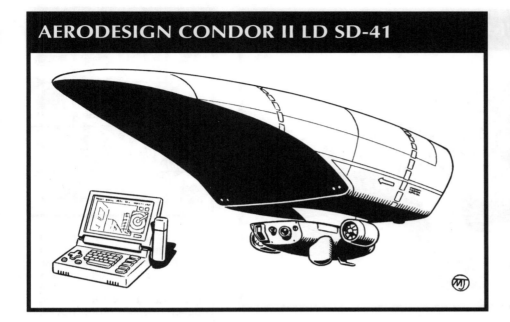

Based on the popular SHAPELY (SHaped Airfoil Positive Enhanced Lift) design, the Condor II drone makes an ideal platform for extended recon and surveillance. This lighter-than-air vehicle requires minimal mechanical lift, reducing its signature and fuel consumption. Modeled on the ground-breaking Condor LDSD-23 drone, the Condor II replaces solar cells with long-duration batteries for extended airtime.

Handling	Speed	B/A	Sig	APilot	Store	Cost
5	30/90	1/3	11	3	4 CF	45,000¥

Economy: 5 km per PF
Power: 25 CFs
Operational Duration: Limited by power
Landing/Takeoff Profile: VSTOL
Set-up/Breakdown Time: 5 minutes
Sensor Package: Standard (I)
Additional Features: Remote-control gear installed. 3 CF available for sensors, ECM/ECCM equipment, or vehicle control gear.

>>>>>(Why risk personnel unless you have to? These days I see plenty of Condors, Condor IIs, and Dalmatians over the battlefield. Well funded units (read: corp) even put up BattleTac™ electronics with a full sensor package. The things you can do with that kind of tactical information!)<<<<<
—Widgit
(04:20:14/12-05-54)

>>>>>(Drones are too vulnerable. Any dog with a rocket can drop them. It's got a good signature, but still makes too easy a target. I stopped using them a few years ago.)<<<<<
—Wombat Warrior
(21:48:39/12-06-54)

>>>>>(Just because drones loiter well doesn't mean you want to limit their movement in such a way. I've seen plenty of poorly trained drone controllers spot a target and circle it while they tell somebody what they've seen. Bad move.)<<<<<
—Matador
(18:20:00/12-07-54)

>>>>>(Always keep your drone moving, even if it's on autopilot.)<<<<<
—Flyer XX
(02:19:10/12-10-54)

STEEL LYNX DRONE

Fighting a dug-in enemy? Send in the Steel Lynx. The Winter Systems Steel Lynx ground-combat drone is a hardened battle machine designed to clear out even the most defensible position. Lightweight, polyceramic armor combines excellent small-arms protection with speed and maneuverability. Arm the Lynx and go hunting!

Handling	Speed	B/A	Sig	APilot	Store	Cost
4/6	40/80	4/12	5	2	20 CF	15,000¥

Economy: 3 km per PF   **Power:** 30 PFs
Operational Duration: Limited by power   **Sensor Package:** Standard (I)
Set-up/Breakdown Time: 3 minutes
Additional Features: Remote-control gear installed. 8 CF available for sensors, ECM/ECCM equipment, vehicle control gear or weapons. Common installations include dedicated hardpoints and a micro-turret that can mount an LMG, HVAR, flechette weapons, and so on. Replaceable power pack costs 3,000¥.

>>>>>(The UCAS military is using more and more Steel Lynxes, testing them as part of mechanized infantry squads where the APC also carries the recharging station and a bunch of spare power packs. Every couple of hours, they pull in the drone and replace the power pack. The controller sits protected in the APC the whole time. Nice system.)<<<<<
—Winter Rat
(06:00:31/12-06-54)

>>>>>(You would know these things, being on the payroll at Winter Systems. <GRIN>)<<<<<
—Hangfire
(21:28:46/12-07-54)

>>>>>(I've never claimed otherwise, have I?)<<<<<
—Winter Rat
(08:20:19/12-09-54)

>>>>>(HEY! They stole my name! I'm gonna sue!!!)<<<<<
—Steel Lynx
(19:10:18/12-10-54)

FERRET RPD-VI PERIMETER DRONE

SALESPERSON

The small, silent Ferret RPD-VI makes the perfect low-maintenance perimeter-security drone. Equipped with sophisticated sensors and a smart autopilot, the Ferret can patrol an area quietly, alert central security when it detects an intruder, and illuminate them with its searchlight or a targeting laser on demand. Use several to cover acres of ground—nothing gets past the Ferret!

Handling	Speed	B/A	Sig	APilot	Store	Cost
3/5	10/30	1/3	8	3	1 CF	154,800¥

Economy: 10 km per PF   **Power:** 10 PF
Operational Duration: Limited by power   **Sensor Package:** Security (I)
Set-up/Breakdown Time: 3 minutes
Additional Features: Remote-control gear installed. 3 CF available for sensors, ECM/ECCM equipment, or vehicle control gear. Also includes white-light searchlight. Laser designator not included (for more information, see p. 85).

>>>>>(Maximum security installations love these things. They lay 'em all over an area, and an intruder can't tell where they'll be because the little bastards wander in random patterns. They're all over the slob who breaks in—lights, lasers, sensors, the works. Next thing the poor slob knows, sentry weapons are opening up from everywhere—with the Ferrets telling the gun where to aim, they ain't gonna miss.)<<<<<
　　—Shadow Vault
　　　　(23:21:01/12-02-54)

>>>>>(Ferrets only matter if you're going in quiet. If it doesn't matter, drop a grenade. Kills them like flies.)<<<<<
　　—Howler
　　　　(20:18:41/12-04-54)

>>>>>(They're useless in the field unless you've got a digital map (softmap) of the area. Without one, the autopilot is near useless. What's the point?)<<<<<
　　—Searcher Stue
　　　　(04:19:18/12-06-54)

WASP/YELLOWJACKET "F" SERIES UPGRADE

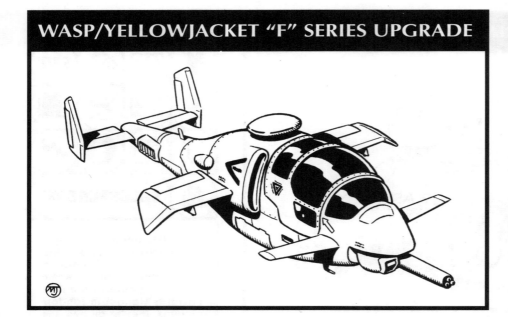

SALESPERSON

After careful analysis of years of field-use and after-action reports, Northrup Industries offers the "F" series upgrade for its PRC-42 Wasp and PRC-44 Yellowjacket light security helicopters. The "F" series offers enhanced small-arms protection, improved handling, engine upgrades to maintain performance, and a reduced signature that makes the Wasp or Yellowjacket a competitor in any market! Fleet-upgrade discounts are available through all Northrup representatives.

	Handling	Sig	B/A	Cost
Wasp Upgrade	−1	+2	2/6	74,000¥
Yellowjacket Upgrade	−1	+2	3/9	110,000¥

For standard Yellowjacket and Wasp statistics, see pp. 70–71, **Rigger Black Book**, or p. 74, **Street Samurai Catalog**.

>>>>>(After-action reports!!! How about "Some kid with a BB gun shot me down?? Or "I'da caught him but he outran me on foot??" Give me a break! These things are like toys; hit them with anything and they fall down. No upgrade can cure that!)<<<<<
—Wylie Eye
(23:28:17/12-06-54)

>>>>(You didn't read the entry very carefully, did you, Wylie? This upgrade lets the Wasp bounce light pistol ammo and absorb the heavier stuff, and the Yellowjacket bounce pretty much everything that classifies as a non-heavy weapon. I'd think twice about playing with these insects.)<<<<<
—Mooch
(10:18:45/12-07-54)

>>>>>(I carry an assault cannon.)<<<<<
—Wylie Eye
(19:02:17/12-08-54)

>>>>>(Oh, well, never mind.)<<<<<
—Mooch
(11:02:18/12-09-54)

VEHICLE SMOKE GENERATOR

Need fast cover? Need a way to break a laser designator's beam? Vehicle smoke generators are the answer to your prayers! Spew smoke on demand from an externally mounted canister that can be triggered from inside the vehicle. Huge, dense clouds cover the battlefield in no time! Special thermal smoke blocks IR-sensing thermographic sensor systems, at only 20 percent over standard costs.

	Number of Charges	Cost
Small Smoke Generator	6	700¥
Large Smoke Generator	12	1,000¥

Each charge covers a given area. For smoke rules, see p. 85.

SALESPERSON

>>>>>(Heh-heh. Reminds me of the time I chased down a well-equipped rebel force in Nicaragua. One of the Appaloosas we were after decided to blow some smoke. The scout was running at more than 100 KPH trailing this long, thin black line. Sensors or no sensors, we could have found the fools by that smoke. Made me laugh.)<<<<<
      —Winter Rat
            (03:20:14/12-07-54)

>>>>>(I know this is off the topic, but don't you guys find it weird to type in a non-written language indicator? Like the "heh-heh" laugh or the <grin> from a few posts back. Isn't it odd typing in body language?)<<<<<
      —Social Adept
            (21:49:30/12-09-54)

>>>>>(Nope. <stupid laugh>)<<<<<
      —Weasel
            (06:28:18/12-10-54)

>>>>>(Never. <schlumping noise>)<<<<<
      —Burrower
            (10:15:17/12-11-54)

ABLATIVE VEHICLE ARMOR

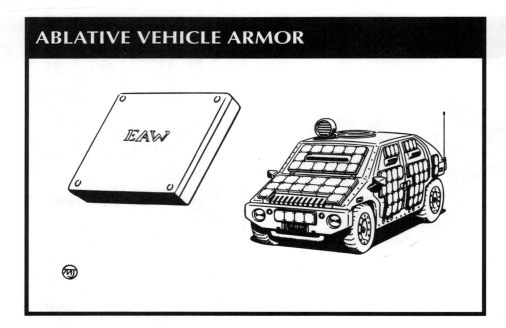

Looking for a little more armor protection for your vehicle? European Arm Works (EAW) has the answer in its new line of modular ablative armor. Designed to attach to the vehicle's exterior, ablative armor absorbs the kinetic energy of any blast. A hit blows the armor plates clear, but they save you from sudden death! Three different available levels let you choose the degree of protection you need! Not usable on aircraft.

Armor Level	Availability	Cost	Street Index
1	8/14 days	700¥	2
2	12/14 days	1,600¥	2
3	14/21 days	2,500¥	2

Ablative armor adds twice its level to a vehicle's effective Armor Rating, to a maximum equal to its Body. When struck by an attack with a Power greater than 3 times the armor level, reduce the increase in the Armor Rating by −1. It takes 6 hours to install ablative armor, which cannot be concealed. Ablative armor is not Hardened. Cost is per point of the vehicle's original body. Also, a motorcycle can only mount up to one-half (round down) of its original Body.

SALESPERSON

>>>>>(Not for the average consumer, but a must-have for the merc or military client in certain environments. We use this armor regularly on supply trucks, cargo haulers, APCs, everything. Works well enough even at the low levels to make it worth the price. Forget low-profile operations, though.)<<<<<
—Winter Rat
(08:28:14/12-05-54)

>>>>>(A good vehicle tech can salvage blown-off armor and reinstall it. I don't know how—you'd have to ask them. I only deride them. <grin>)<<<<<
—Loodles
(23:48:30/12-06-54)

>>>>>(I've seen the low levels of ablative armor on choppers and such. Wreaks havoc with aerodynamics and stability, but it does the job it's designed to do.)<<<<<
—Fly Boy
(19:12:02/12-07-54)

>>>>>(And it blows fragments into the rotor when hit. Dumb idea.)<<<<<
—Matador
(03:29:12/12-08-54)

RULES

This section offers combat rules expansions, clarifications, and options in response to player and gamemaster questions and comments. An expanded Weapon Range Table that provides ranges for all **Shadowrun** weapons published to date, including the new weapons described in this book, appears at the end of this section.

DEVELOPER NOTES

This sourcebook exposes and explains the shadowy realm of the mercenary. This sourcebook is not about playing a mercenary storyline, but about playing a mercenary character within the **Shadowrun** storyline. In the former case, all the player characters are mercenaries and the story objectives have purely mercenary origins and direction. In the latter, the mercenary player character plays a specific part shaped by his unique experiences, viewpoint, and attitude. Creative gamemasters may find enough information in this sourcebook to create a "mercs-only" spin-off of **Shadowrun**, but this book was not designed with that outcome in mind. (Good luck, though, to those who decide to go for it!)

This book also includes plenty of gear. Mercs like toys as much as street samurai do, and this book presents a hefty cross-section of useful, fun equipment. As one might expect, the classifications of merc toys and street sam toys overlap pretty far. After all, it isn't really, "He who dies with the most toys wins," but, "He who uses his toys best wins." Some equipment described in this book duplicates information and gear from previous **Shadowrun** products, because feedback from **Shadowrun** players and gamemasters indicated that the public wanted more information about a specific item or a game mechanic related to that item's use. To make life easier for players and gamemasters, both existing and new information has been grouped into one place.

With regard to the rules expansions, clarifications, and combat options offered in this section, FASA sends abject apologies to those who might have received conflicting adjudications to these rules questions some time in the past.

CHOOSING OPTIONAL RULES

Consider all the rules clarifications, expansions, and options in this sourcebook as optional suggestions for play. As always, gamemasters and players should review these rules before beginning play and agree on which ones to use. The gamemaster and players are also the final arbiters of how rules should be interpreted.

EXPANSIONS AND CLARIFICATIONS

The following expansions and clarifications refer to the existing rules printed in **Shadowrun, Second Edition** (1992). Page references for that book are provided where necessary.

ARMOR DEGRADATION

For the sake of simplified bookkeeping, **SRII** ignored the effects of armor degradation. The following rule takes armor degradation into account.

A character who takes a Moderate wound or greater damage from a non-Stun attack suffers armor damage. The armor loses 1 point for every multiple of its appropriate value represented by the Power of the attack. For example, a character wearing an armored jacket takes a hit from a submachine gun burst with a Damage Code of 10S. The jacket has a Ballistic Rating of 5. If the character takes at least Moderate damage, the attack permanently reduces the rating of the armor by 2 points.

This rule also applies to Impact armor. Hardened body or vehicle armor (but not critter armor) degrades at the same rate.

ATHLETIC TESTS

The following rules apply to resolving Athletics Tests, specifically for running, jumping, climbing, swimming and so on. Some of the material below first appeared in **SRII** and other sources. In all instances, Damage Modifiers (p. 112, **SRII**) apply.

Climbing

Characters normally perform one of two types of climbing: unassisted and assisted. Unassisted climbing is exactly what it sounds like—the character climbs on the strength of his or her own ability. Assisted climbing involves the use of climbing equipment.

Make the Climbing Test (requiring a Complex Action) against a target number reflecting the difficulty of the obstacle being climbed. The gamemaster determines the base target number by how easy the surface is to climb (craggy, sheer, and so on), modified by the height of the obstacle and the current environmental conditions.

CLIMBING TABLE	
Condition	**Target Number**
Easily climbable surface (i.e., chain link fence)	3
Broken surface (i.e., debris, tree, loose stone wall)	5
Flat surface (i.e., brick wall, side of old building)	8
Sheer surface (i.e., metal wall, seamless stone)	14
Height:	**Modifier**
less than 2 meters	No modifier
2–4 meters	+2
4+ meters	+4
Obstacle is slippery or wet	+2
Obstacle is greased, gel-treated, and so on	+4

Characters can normally climb upward a number of meters each turn equal to one-quarter (25 percent) the average of their Quickness and Strength (round down). For each success from the Climbing Test, add 2 to the average of Quickness and Strength for this calculation. Climbing down is easier: characters can move down a number of meters equal to twice the average of their Quickness and Strength. (Characters can, of course, elect to climb down *really* quickly. See **Falling** rules, p. 76.)

Assisted climbing makes the upward climb slower, but allows the character to overcome the conditions listed in the Climbing Table. Assisted climbing requires the use of climbing gear (see **Field Pack**, p. 56). When using climbing gear, modify the base target number for the Climbing Test by −10, making a Climbing Test once every three minutes to reflect the time it takes to safely position the climbing gear on the surface being climbed.

Assisted climbing down, known as rappelling, is *a lot* faster. With the proper equipment, rappelling allows characters to make a controlled descent at close to free-fall speeds and introduces the handy ability to slow the descent and land safely. A rappelling character falls at a rate of 20 meters per Simple Action expended. Note that only one of the two Simple Actions available in a Combat Phase can be expended in this manner. Yes, this means that a character can rappel and shoot in the same Action Phase, but must add a +4 modifier to both the Firearms Test and the Climbing Test.

Rappelling characters increase the number of meters descended that Action Phase by 1 for each success from a Climbing (4) Test. When the character reaches the bottom (or his destination), he must make another Climbing (4) Test. On an unsuccessful test, the character falls 4 meters and takes appropriate damage. See **Falling**, below.

If the Rule of One applies during any Climbing Test, the character plummets the full distance to the ground. Benevolent gamemasters may allow the character to make a Quickness (6) Test to grab something and prevent the fall.

Falling

All falls have a Damage Level of "D", with the Power of the fall's "attack" being one-half the number of meters fallen (round down). The character may use Body dice for a Damage Resistance Test to reduce the damage. Subtract one-half (round down) of the character's impact armor rating from the Power of the fall. Characters may also make an Athletics Test against a target number equal to the full distance fallen (in meters). Each success from this test also reduces the Power of the fall by 1.

A falling character has a "Falling Action" every 10 Combat Phases. At that time the character is considered to have fallen a number of additional meters equal to 20 meters times the number of "Falling Actions" (including the current one) spent in rapid descent. A falling character has an Initiative of 30 for every turn until the character lands.

For those gamemasters counting in real-time, remember that a falling body plummets at an acceleration rate of about 10 meters/per second/per second. The falling character drops 10 meters in the first second, 20 more meters in the second, 30 more meters in the third, and so on. The reason for the difference in the falling rate values (20 in **SRII** rules and 10 in real life) is that the **SRII** Combat Turn takes up an abstract amount of time of between 3 and 5 seconds, depending on what happens. The 20 value seemed like a good compromise. Feel free to modify it, however.

Holding One's Breath

A character can hold his or her breath for 30 seconds for each point of his or her Body. A character who wants to hold his breath longer makes a Body (4) Test. Each success increases the length of time the character can hold his breath by 10 percent (round down).

Jumping

Characters can make four types of jumps: standing jumps, running jumps, standing vertical jumps, and running vertical jumps. From a standing start, a character can jump a number of meters equal to his one-half his Strength, minus his natural Body (unaugmented by cyberware, bioware, or magic) minimum one meter. For a running jump, the character may add his Quickness (Quickness + Strength − Body ÷ 2 = meters jumped).

Use the same formulas for jumping vertically from a standing or running start, but divide the result by 4.

To increase the distance jumped, a character makes a Jumping Test against a target number equal to the number of meters the character is trying to clear. Each success increases the distance jumped by 10 percent (round down).

A failed jump or a jump down may result in falling (see **Falling**, p. 76).

Lifting/Throwing

A character can lift 25 kilograms per point of his Strength without making any sort of test. To represent augmented strength, the character makes a Strength Test against a target number equal to the weight of the object being lifted, divided by 10 (round up). Each success increases the weight lifted by 10 percent (round down). Note that this rule applies to a simple lift off the ground. A character can only lift over his head an object that weighs 12 kilograms per point of Strength. In this case, apply the Strength Test normally.

Once a character lifts an object over his head, he can throw that object a number of meters equal to the character's Strength, minus the object's weight divided by 50 (round down). To increase the distance thrown, make a Strength Test against a target number equal to the weight of the object being lifted divided by 10 (round up). For every 2 successes, the object flies an additional meter.

Running

The Movement rules appear on p. 83, **SRII.** Characters with the Running Skill may attempt to increase the distance they can run by spending a Complex Action (Use Skill). Each success against a Target Number of 4 increases the character's effective Quickness by 1 point for that Combat Phase. The gamemaster may apply modifiers for various types of terrain (slippery, rocky, and so on) and other conditions.

Swimming

Use the same rules to determine swimming speed and distance as for running, except divide all resulting distances by 4.

BATTLETAC™ SYSTEM

The most straightforward way to explain the benefits of the BattleTac™ and similar systems is to say that everyone using the system can freely exchange various types of data and information without restriction. This data may include map positioning, enemy positioning, current status, targeting data, video and aural information, tactical requests and commands, and anything else of import to the soldier.

When the system is operating, any piece of data known to one member of the "battle network" is known to all. For example, if one soldier sees an advancing enemy unit, all others in the "network" instantly know that force's composition, direction, heading, and speed. Other members in the network can use this data as spotting information and call for indirect fire against that target, or maneuver to intercept or ambush those forces. Because all members of the BattleTac™ unit see all information simultaneously, the unit can move like a well-programmed machine and react quickly to changing battlefield conditions.

The BattleTac™ system works in a manner similar to the telecommunication system described on p. xx. Use the ratings given for that system to represent signal security and encryption efficiency. If a system has BattleTac™ capability, multiply all prices by 10.

CAMOUFLAGE AND PERCEPTION

The modifiers given below apply to visual Perception Tests made to detect opponents wearing camouflage clothing. A moving character qualifies for the "Action very obvious" modifier (see p. 185, **SRII**).

Situation	Modifier
Appropriate camouflage clothing (i.e., woodland in the woods)	+4
Inappropriate camouflage clothing (i.e., desert in the woods)	−2

CASED VS. CASELESS AMMO

The **Shadowrun** rules and fiction occasionally mention caseless ammunition. Caseless ammunition is made without a brass or plastic casing holding the propellant. Instead, the propellant is a solid mass attached to the tail of the bullet, and burns completely away when fired. Caseless ammunition exists in fact as well as in fiction. The following rules apply to caseless ammo.

•For the sake of simplicity, assume that any modern firearm (post-2050) can be acquired in a model that fires caseless ammunition. Increase the base cost by 50 percent and the Availability by +1.

•Caseless ammunition is available at 150 percent of the base cost. Increase the Availability by +1.

•Caseless ammunition takes up slightly less space than cased ammunition. Increase the number of rounds a caseless weapon can load by 20 percent (round down). Caseless ammo also weighs less, so reduce the appropriate weights by 20 percent (round up).

•Caseless ammunition cannot be used in a weapon designed to fire cased ammunition, and vice versa.

All other normal firearms rules apply.

COMBAT ACCIDENTS

The following variant on the Rule of One creates a greater chance of provoking accidental mayhem in combat. In ranged or melee combat, if the player rolls all of his dice (Skill dice, Combat Pool dice, Enhancement dice, everything) and achieves a number of ones equal to or greater than the number of base Skill dice used for the test, the result is an "Oops." The gamemaster determines the appropriate "Oops" for each situation. For inspiration, see the **Stray Shots** optional rule, p. 93, **SRII**. The character may also break, jam, or drop his weapon. Be creative.

Yes, the character can spend Karma to avoid the "Oops" per the rules given on p. 191, **SRII**.

COVER MODIFIERS

The **SRII** rules for ranged combat offer only a rudimentary modifier for obscured targets, called Partial Cover (–4). The following optional rules expand the uses of that modifier.

Attacking characters who want to use cover to protect against return fire may choose the amount of cover they use, represented by a +2, +4, or +6 modifier. The attacking character must also modify the target number by one-half the cover modifier. For example, a character partially concealing himself behind +4 cover must add a +2 modifier to his attack because of that cover. (Hey, hiding is awkward for you, too.)

Gamemasters may need to determine the amount of cover protecting a target, especially when that cover is environmental and coincidental (characters fighting in the woods, an amusement park, and so on). The gamemaster should base the modifier on how much of the target is visible, using the Partial Cover Table below as a guideline.

The gamemaster should judge how much of the target can be seen in terms of an overall area. For example, if the gamemaster judges that the various areas of the target (big and small) that can be seen through the brush totals about 48.5 percent, the modifier would be +4.

PARTIAL COVER TABLE	
Percent of Target Visible	Modifier
76–100	No modifier
51–75	+2
26–50	+4
1–25	+6
0	+8 (Blind Fire)

COVERING/SUPPRESSION FIRE

A character may declare that he is making a ranged attack to provide covering/suppression fire. This means that the attacker is directing fire into an area to force his opponents to keep their heads down for fear of being hit. Covering/suppression fire usually allows the character's teammates to perform some action unopposed.

Each round fired effectively covers a 1-meter area for 10 Combat Phases. Multiple rounds may be targeted at a single 1-meter area to increase the effectiveness of the covering/suppression fire. If the attack covers multiple areas, these areas must be directly adjacent to another covered area.

If, during the time that the area is covered, a character enters that area, moves, and thereby exposes himself to the covering/suppression fire, or presents his body to fire within that area in any manner, he might be hit. If line of sight can be drawn from the attacker to any part of the target during the time the area is covered, the target is potentially vulnerable.

To determine if the covering/suppression fire strikes the target character, resolve a Ranged Attack against the target by rolling a number of dice equal to the number of rounds fired at the area. The Target Number equals a base of 4 modified only by Cover and any Damage Modifier the attacker must add. Every 2 successes generated results in 1 round striking the target, up to a maximum of the number of rounds fired into the area.

CUSTOM WEAPONS

The owner of a weapon can customize its grip and balance at a cost of 100 percent of the base weapon cost. The work takes a weaponsmith approximately three days to complete. A weapon customized for a particular character allows him to roll an additional skill die when using this weapon. A character who uses a weapon customized for someone else must subtract 1 die from his skill roll.

DELAYED ACTIONS AND SHORT MOVES

Characters who choose to Delay their Action may move up to one-half (round up) their Walking rate during the Combat Phase of their original Initiative. When the character makes the Delayed Action, he may move normally.

Josh, a street samurai, is slowly advancing down a corridor, watching the door at the end. His Initiative is 23, and so he Delays his action in Combat Phase 23. At that time, he moves 3 meters down the corridor (half his normal walking movement). His next action would normally take place in Combat Phase 13. He maintains the Delayed Action, but advances another 3 meters at that time. He continues to Delay his actions and move until he reaches the door.

DELAYED GRENADE RULES

Shadowrun grenades can be fired, scatter, and detonate all within one Combat Phase (a fraction of a second). The system resolves grenade attacks in this manner simply to cut down on the bookkeeping required. Ambitious gamemasters and players may want to apply the following delayed grenade rule.

Grenades detonate 5 Combat Phases after firing. During that time another character with an available action (either a Delayed Action or normal Initiative) may retrieve the grenade and attempt to throw it back. Characters must achieve at least 1 success on a Quickness (8) Test to pick up a bouncing, jumping, skittering, mini-grenade. To pick up a regular-sized grenade, characters must make a successful Quickness (6) Test. If the test is unsuccessful, the character is at an effective Range of 0 when the grenade detonates.

Have fun!

INSTANT DEATH AND OVER-DAMAGE

As written, the **SRII** rules make it effectively impossible to kill an unwounded character with a single attack. In fact, an unwounded character can technically survive a nuclear blast at ground zero, because the nuke only does "D" damage with no Body Overflow. Though such a result may look like an oversight, it was a deliberate choice to avoid the potential disappointment of having a player character taken down by a single attack, especially an unexpected attack or one against which the character cannot defend himself. In certain situations, however, this choice becomes ludicrous. In these cases, apply the following rule.

Normally, after a weapon's Damage Level has been staged up to "D," additional successes are ignored. If the Power of the attack is greater than twice (2x) the Body Rating of the target, the gamemaster may invoke the Over-Damage rule. With this rule, every 2 additional successes translate into 1 additional point of damage applied against the Physical Condition Monitor (if the attack was Deadly Stun) or Body Overflow (if the attack was Deadly Physical). For example, using the Over-Damage rule, assume a character with a Body of 3 is struck by a 7M attack. The attacker stages the damage for a final Damage Level of Deadly, with an additional 4 successes remaining in the attacker's favor. The character takes a Deadly wound and 2 points of Body Overflow, leaving him with 1 point remaining and ten minutes until he bleeds to death. If the attacker had achieved 2 additional successes, the poor character would be instantly dead.

Use this rule cautiously: in addition to conveniently killing those nasty bad guys, this rule handily kills favorite player characters who might otherwise have narrowly survived to run the shadows another day.

LOW-LIGHT AND THERMAL SYSTEMS

The following information elaborates on the fundamental characteristics, differences, and capabilities of low-light and thermographic systems. Theory and application has been streamlined for simplicity and playability.

Low-Light Systems

Also known as night sight, night vision, or light amplification, low-light systems involve an electronic process that creates a coherent electronic image by amplifying and processing even the tiniest amount of available light. If no light is available, however, even the best low-light system becomes useless.

The gamemaster has the final say on whether a situation offers sufficient light for a low-light system to work. He or she simply decides if light is present. If not, then the low-light system has no light to amplify and therefore has no effect. If light is present, even in such faint sources as moonlight leaking through low cloud cover or traces of a streetlight filtering into an abandoned basement, then the low-light system has something to amplify.

The low-light system itself can provide the light required for its use as either direct or area lighting. For example, direct lighting could come from a penlight that throws a focused beam of light. Even the tiniest glow from a penlight, which cannot be seen from more than a few meters away, can illuminate a map, a sign, or similar small area or object well enough to create an image on the system's screen. Characters who carry low-light systems usually attach a penlight or similar pinpoint light source to a helmet or their finger to provide direct, subtle illumination on demand.

An area light combined with a low-light system is sufficient to allow the person so equipped to move. This light need not cover a large area; it could be as directional as a flashlight that subtly illuminates the area ahead of the user. Such a light will be visible for some distance, but only if the observer is looking into the beam.

Low-light systems are technologically based, and so magic cannot be cast through them. The nature of low-light vision requires an electronic amplification of light, by definition a translation of the image to electronic form. Because low-light cybereyes have been paid for with Essence, however, the system becomes an accepted part of a character's body and can be used to cast magic. Optical low-light systems use high-quality optics, lenses, and/or mirrors rather than electronic imaging. Their light-gathering capabilities are limited by the size of the gathering lens. Effectively fancy telescopes, optical low-light systems are not portable.

Thermographic Systems

Thermographic systems read heat (infrared energy) emitted by a target. This type of system provides few details about the target, because it reveals only degrees of heat. **SRII** assumes that modern (2050) thermal systems actually superimpose the thermographic display over a basic, amplified low-light display for better detail. The result provides insufficient data to gain a bonus or modifier, but does allow the user to navigate past obstacles or differentiate between objects while using the system.

Different systems use different color scales to represent the levels of heat, but most use the following standard. Hot objects (an engine block, a pot of boiling water) show as white, while cool objects (room temperature) show as black, with every temperature difference in between displaying as shades of red or green. Remember that the system judges "hot" and "cold" in relation to the local air or room temperature. For example, thermographic systems used outside in the winter easily spot a person or vehicle, because they will appear "hot" compared to the air temperature. On the other hand, in the rain forests of South America little difference exists between the ambient temperature (the forest's "room temperature") and the radiated body heat of a human being, making thermographic systems all but

useless for differentiating between the forest and a person. (Odds are that motion will give the target away, but that's a different modifier.)

When characters are using thermographic systems, the gamemaster must consider the relative temperature of objects viewed against the ambient temperature to determine if the system detects the target. In other words, objects at a similar temperature show up on the display as similar colors, making it difficult to differentiate between them if they overlap.

By definition, thermographic systems also require technology and cannot be used when casting magic. Because the user has paid Essence for thermographic cybereyes, however, the system becomes an accepted part of a character's body and can be used to cast magic.

Natural Low-Light and Thermal Vision

Natural low-light or thermographic vision, such as the vision elves and dwarfs are born with, or the enhanced senses available to a physical adept or critter, is magical in nature. This type of vision works along principles similar to those of low-light and thermographic systems, but performs better than any technology can. Though a certain biological basis exists to explain this visual ability, much of the effect can only be explained through the application of magic.

Natural low-light or thermographic vision is assumed to be always operating, providing vision enhancements automatically as needed. For example, a troll sees exactly what humans see when looking at the same view, except that every object, person, and so on is tinged with the heat it radiates. The hotter an object, the more brilliant the color the troll sees. Objects that are much hotter than their environment appear whiter, surrounded by a faint glow. Trolls see this way normally, and therefore can instantly perceive, process, and interpret what they see. Natural low-light or thermal vision is an advantage, not a handicap.

MAXIMUM RATE OF FIRE

The following information offers a comprehensive version of the **Shadowrun** maximum rate of weapon fire.

•Regular weapons capable of burst-fire (see p.92, **SRII**) fire 3 rounds per burst. A character can fire these rounds twice within a Combat Phase (See **Fire Weapon**, p.82, **SRII**).

•Regular weapons capable of full-auto fire (see pp. 92–93, **SRII**) can fire *up to* 10 rounds in 1 Combat Phase. The firer may use these 10 rounds to make as many full-auto bursts of between 3 and 10 rounds per burst as he wishes, up to a maximum of 10 total rounds that Combat Phase.

•Minigun-class weapons can fire up to 15 rounds per Combat Phase using the full-auto mode rules (pp. 92–93, **SRII**). The weapon always fires 15 rounds if those rounds are available.

•Super machinegun-class weapons (new to this sourcebook) fire a maximum of 15 rounds per Combat Phase. They fire six-round bursts in burst-fire mode, and full-auto bursts of between 6 and 15 rounds per burst, up to a maximum of 15 rounds per Combat Phase.

The **Shadowrun** Combat Turn does not limit the maximum number of rounds that a weapon can discharge within that turn. The cyclic or recycle rates of the various weapons are assumed to be high enough to support the rates of fire cited above. A modern-day submachine gun has a cyclic rate of 600 rounds per minute, or 10 rounds per second. **Shadowrun** weapons have lower cyclic rates in the interests of game balance, practicality, survivability, and sanity.

MERCENARY CONTACTS

The mercenary equivalent of the fixer, known as the dealer (same game statistics, different area of influence), serves as the merc's source for weapons and equipment. Even more so than the fixer, the dealer traffics regularly in arms and accessories and therefore can more easily get merc-related equipment, though the player character must wait longer to receive it. The dealer has more pipelines to work through than the fixer does, but the flow is slower.

To reflect this fact, decrease the target numbers for acquisition through a dealer by –1 and increase the Time Required by 25 percent (round down). The dealer contact should only be available to characters with a legitimate mercenary background. Gamemasters should enforce this restriction to maintain game balance. Only legitimate current or past members of the League can work with a dealer.

OFF-HAND TRAINING

Off-hand training represents a character's ambidextrous ability acquired through the Special Skill: Ambidexterity. A character can only acquire this skill during character creation. It cannot be learned during game play. This Special Skill costs 2 Skill Points per point of Skill Rating. The Skill Rating can later be increased using the normal rules for increasing a General Skill (p.190, **SRII**).

This Special Skill is used in a unique way. Any time the character attempts to use his off-hand (non-dominant hand), he must apply a negative modifier to the target number equal to the appropriate Skill Rating, minus the Special Skill. So, a character with a Firearms Skill of 5 and Ambidexterity of 3 attempting to shoot with her off-hand must apply a +2 (5 – 3) modifier. An Ambidexterity Skill Rating higher than the rating of the skill being used has no effect.

When using multiple firearms, characters must also apply the **Using A Second Firearm** modifier (p. 90, **SRII**).

Second Weapon In Melee Combat

Characters may learn armed melee combat styles that allow them to use a second weapon. The following rules represent the effects of using a second melee weapon in combat.

•The second weapon must be physically smaller and lighter than the dominant weapon, unless they are both small weapons (such as knives or daggers).

•The character must know how to use each of the two weapons individually. (Yes, they may both fall under the general skill Armed Combat.)

•The character must acquire a Special Skill for the fighting style (Rapier and Dagger, and so on).

A character using two weapons in combat makes his Attack Test by rolling a base number of dice equal to the character's combined individual skills in the two weapons. The character may add a number of Combat Pool dice up to a maximum equal to the Special Skill rating.

Resolve damage by finding the average of the two weapons used. First, calculate an unmodified average of the Power of both weapons. If one weapon has a higher Damage Level than the other, subtract 1 level from the higher Damage Level and use the result as the Damage. For example, a character using a sword with an "M" Damage Level and a knife with an "L" Damage Level would use an "L" Damage Level.

Resolve the use of both weapons with a single test using the Power calculated above. Remember that **Shadowrun** melee combat is not resolved blow by blow.

Instead, each Attack Test is an abstraction or amalgamation of a series of moves, blows, feints, parries, and countermoves. All other melee combat rules apply normally.

The stats for typical weapons used in two-weapon combat appear below, abstracted in order to avoid printing a list of virtually identical weapons differentiated only by their names.

Weapon	Concealability	Reach	Damage	Weight	Cost
Light Sword	4	1	(Str + 1) M	.75	700¥
Long Knife/ Dagger	6	0	(Str + 2) L	.5	150¥

PHYSICAL AND STUN DAMAGE

Characters may use weapons listed as inflicting Stun Damage to inflict Physical Damage, such as clubs, fists, and so on. A character who wishes to inflict Physical Damage using a weapon normally rated as doing Stun Damage must add a +4 modifier to the target number. The Damage Code of the weapon remains the same, but the attack results in Physical Damage rather than Stun Damage.

PULLING PUNCHES

Characters in melee combat can elect to "pull their punches." To pull a punch, the player must state how many successes are being "pulled" to lessen the blow before the Attack Test is resolved. Increase the target number by +1 and resolve the test normally. Determine the total number of successes, then subtract the number of successes being "pulled" from that value. Make this calculation as soon as the successes are generated, but before comparing the attacker's total successes to the opponent's total successes.

Characters can also choose to decrease the effect of a ranged attack. To do this, add a +4 modifier to the target number, then follow the rules given above.

RECOIL AND STRENGTH

The following rule suggests a way to allow characters who possess extraordinary Strength to suffer less from firearm recoil than characters with standard Strength. Because many characters with high Strength Ratings rely heavily on firearms, this rule makes the game even deadlier. (The troll carrying the light machine gun should love this rule.)

RECOIL REDUCTION TABLE	
Strength	**Recoil Reduction**
1–4	None
5–6	–1
7–8	–2
9–10	–3
11–12	–4

For every 2 full points of a character's Strength Rating above 3, the character gains 1 level of Recoil Reduction, as shown on the Recoil Reduction Table below.

SENSOR TARGETING OF HUMANS

Vehicle sensors can target people using an effective Signature of 8. See **Sensor-Enhanced Targeting**, p.106, **Rigger Black Book**.

SENTRY GUNS

The Sentry™ system uses microtronic technology similar to the tactical computer found on p. 53, **Shadowtech**. A tactical computer is a dedicated system designed to keep track of all relevant combat data. The computer derives its information from all available sensing devices, which means it is not foolproof. If the sensor cannot provide the appropriate information, the computer may not be able to make correct decisions. Each individual extra sensor type (low-light, audio, ultrasound) increases the tactical computer's Level by 1. Access to a digital softmap of the area adds 2 to the tactical computer's Intelligence.

A tactical computer can keep track of, or "mark," and predict movements of a number of targets equal to its Intelligence Rating. To successfully mark a target, the tactical computer must make a Success Test pitting its Intelligence against a target number based on the range to the target (using standard shotgun ranges). Apply all appropriate situation modifiers for ranged combat (p. 88–90, **SRII**). The extra successes generated for each target serve as the system's Success Level for that target.

The target can shake the computer's marking by breaking out of the Sentry system's line of sight. Doing so forces the computer to attempt to re-acquire the target when the target becomes visible again. To attempt to reacquire the target, roll a number of dice equal to the system's Intelligence against a Base Target Number 1, modified by +1 for every meter the target moved while out of line of sight and +1 for every full Combat Turn that has passed. If this test succeeds, the Success Level for that target is now based on the successes generated in the test. If the test is unsuccessful, the computer can attempt to re-mark the target on the system's next action. An accurate map of the area in computer memory or accessible over a data network (gamemaster's discretion) reduces the target number of the Re-acquisition Test by –3.

The targeting feature and trajectory computation adds an additional number of dice equal to the previously generated Success Level for a target to all Ranged Combat Success Tests against that target. This modifier applies only to those targets marked by the tactical system.

All system functions are background tasks, requiring no actions to call up or perform. Though an attempt at a new marking after a failed re-acquisition does not cost

an action, the computer can only attempt a new marking during the system's action.

When the Sentry™ system fires on a target, use a Skill Rating of 5, adding the following modifiers if using the Enhanced Targeting option: +1 Enhanced Targeting is installed and an additional +1 per additional integrated sensor. Resolve this combat per the normal rules.

SHOTGUN SOUND SUPPRESSION

Practically speaking, shotguns cannot use a silencer or the rules that apply to it. A character using a shotgun firing only slug rounds rather than shot/flechette rounds, however, can install a sound suppresser. A shotgun equipped with sound suppression cannot fire shot/flechette rounds that use or require a choke.

A shotgun blast is the aural equivalent of full-auto fire. Shotguns that can fire in burst or full-auto modes cannot be equipped with a sound suppresser.

SMALL UNIT TACTICS

Characters with the Military Science Skill (ideally coupled with the Small Unit Tactics Specialization) can gain an Initiative bonus for their teammates under certain circumstances. The character with Small Unit Tactics must make his or her last action of the Combat Turn a Complex Action (Skill Use), even if he or she has only one action available. The character then makes the Skill Test against a base Target Number of 4, with the following considerations and modifiers.

•The character with tactical skill must be in contact or communication with everyone who is to receive the Initiative bonus.

•If the character with tactical skill has only radio (or similar) communication with his team members, add a +2 modifier to the Skill Test target number.

•If all members of the team are linked by the BattleTac™ system (see **Field Pack**, p. 59) or another similar system, apply a –2 modifier.

•Apply all appropriate Damage Modifiers.

Team members in communication with the character possessing tactical skill receive a bonus to their Initiative for the next Combat Turn equal to +1 for every 2 successes the tactical character generates. The tactical character may add Karma Pool dice to his Skill Test.

This bonus also applies in surprise and ambush situations. See p. 86, **SRII**.

SMARTLINK LEVEL II

The Smartlink Level II hardware and software represents an evolutionary increase in smartgun technology. Most of the changes have no effect in game terms; the Smartlink simply feels better and works more efficiently. Smartlink Level II offers the following game system benefits.

•Smartlink Level II software can integrate with a rangefinder to provide an additional –1 target modifier at long range and a –2 target modifier at extreme range.

•Called Shots (p. 92, **SRII**) are easier to make with Smartlink Level II. Apply a +2 Called Shot modifier when using Smartlink Level II.

•Smartlink Level II can calculate indirect-fire arcs, applying a –1 modifier for linked weapons such as under-barrel grenade launchers, grenade guns, and the like. This benefit also applies to rocket launchers and similar systems, but not to missile launchers and other systems with an inherent Intelligence Rating.

SMOKE RULES

Smoke can be deployed using a grenade or other smoke-producing device. The amount of smoke produced is limited by the size of the device used. How long the smoke lasts depends on the environment.

If the smoke is deployed in an area with no wind, the smoke lingers in the area of impact until the duration expires. If the smoke is deployed in an area with wind, the smoke cloud will stretch and thin out in the direction the wind is blowing. Gamemasters can use the Scatter diagram (p. 97, **SRII**) to determine wind direction. To determine wind speed, roll one six-sided die. The duration of a blowing smoke cloud is found by subtracting the result of the wind strength D6 from 7, and in turn dividing that number into the indicated duration for the smoke. (So, for example, a smoke mortar round explodes. Scatter (wind direction) is determined. Then another D6 is rolled for wind strength; the result is 5 (a strong wind). Therefore, the smoke will only remain, blowing and dissipating in the direction of the wind, for 7 - 5=2, 4 ÷ 2=2 minutes before it offers no modifier. If the characters involved are exchanging gunfire or attempting to observe something, the gamemaster must determine on a case-by-case basis whether the characters can see through an area of thinning smoke (Light Smoke per p. 89, **SRII**) or if the bulk of the smoke obstructs their actions (Heavy Smoke per p. 89, **SRII**).

SMOKE TABLE

Type	Area of Effect	Duration (in minutes)	Additional Effects
Grenade	10m radius	2	Obscures vision (p. 89, **SRII**)
Mortar	15m radius	4	Obscures vision (p. 89, **SRII**)
Vehicle	10m radius cloud or 10 x 5 x 4m ribbon	4	Obscures vision (p. 89, **SRII**)
Thermal	—	—	Contains hot particles, obscures thermographic vision (p. 89, **SRII**)

TARGET DESIGNATORS

Target designators mark a target and assist in aiming. The simplest target designator is the laser sight, which emits a beam of visible laser light that strikes the target and marks it with a red dot. The dot lets the firer know exactly where he or she is aiming and allows him to adjust the shot.

All target designators operate on variations of this principle. With regard to more complicated designators, the individual using the target designator is not the individual firing the weapon; that individual could be kilometers away. The weapon may even be automated and fired by remote command. The two basic types of target designators are laser sights and reflected-energy designators.

Laser Sight

The basic laser sight described on p. 240, **SRII** can mark a target with a visible red dot at a distance of up to 500 meters at night and 50 meters during the day. Smoke and other environmental conditions, however, may block this laser sight. Divide the listed range by 2 for light rain, mist, or fog, by 4 for heavy rain, mist, fog, or smoke, and by 10 for downpours and very thick smoke. To find a laser sight's day range under these conditions, divide the listed night range by 10. Characters using a laser sight gain a –1 modifier to their ranged combat target number if they can see the dot.

The high-powered laser sight is a more powerful version of the basic sight. It offers a night range of 1,500 meters and a day range of 150 meters. The same environment and target modifier rules apply.

Reflected-Energy Designators

A reflected-energy designator effectively functions as an even higher-powered laser sight, but serves a different purpose. A designator is designed to mark a target with reflected energy such as laser light, microwave, or radar. A weapon with the appropriate tracking/seeker head can then home in on this reflected energy.

In all cases, the weapon skill of the character using the designator determines whether the weapon (regardless of the type) hits the target. Weapons that home in on designated targets require that the designator keep the beam (laser, microwave, or radar) on the target. For laser designators (which can be top-mounted on a rifle-sized weapon), the designating character uses the Firearms (Rifle) Skill. For microwave or radar designators, use the character's Gunnery Skill. All normal ranged combat rules apply, but consult the Weapon Range Table on p. 87 of this book for the designator in use. Note that microwave and radar designators can be mounted on a tripod for field use or vehicle mounted. (To mount one on a vehicle requires 1 CF of cargo area; see p. 113, **Rigger Black Book**.)

Smoke blocks laser designators, and chaff blocks microwave and radar designators. For game purposes, assume that the mere presence of smoke or chaff intervening between the target and the designator blocks the beam. (Reality is more complex, but this rule is not intended as a military simulation.) The gamemaster must determine on a case-by-case basis the location of emitted smoke or chaff in relation to the position of the designator. Also, for the sake of simplicity, assume that all missile or rocket weapons have a flight-time of 1,000 meters per Combat Turn.

TELECOMMUNICATIONS SYSTEMS

The Phillips Tacticom system described on p. 58 of this book is a sophisticated piece of military electronics. The statistics for the system, however, are also representative of other brands and systems that serve a similar function. For example, the statistics for the two master units work equally well for vehicle systems, the larger master unit available for vehicles with the available space (or budget), and the smaller, lighter portable master unit fitting into vehicles that offer less room.

This equipment conforms with the **Using Equipment** rules, p. 184, **SRII**. It has an ECM/ECCM Rating equal to the rating of the equipment.

The large master unit has a tactical range of 30 kilometers, the portable master unit a range of 20 kilometers. The manufacturer designed the Tacticom system with this short range to ensure signal security and reduce the probability of long-range detection. Communication is two-way voice-only. The master units are encrypted at the rating of the equipment.

Individual team members carry the system's personal comm unit: with a range of 12 kilometers, also made deliberately short for greater security. Note that beyond 12 kilometers these units can receive messages from a master unit, but cannot respond.

The microwave link is a small, flat-transmitter microwave system that provides greater signal security by virtue of its position at line-of-sight to the horizon. This same feature also creates a disadvantage because the user must be able to trace a direct line of sight between the link's sender and receiver. The microwave signal is only marginally affected by weather, and can only be intercepted by someone or something lying on or very close to the path of the microwave beam. Because the real workings of microwave communication systems and other systems equally subtle and involved are beyond the effective scope of **Shadowrun**, gamemasters should use these guidelines to rule on the many and varied circumstances that are bound to arise during play.

The laser link works on a principle similar to the microwave link, except that communication relies on a laser beam. This system also requires a direct line of sight, but a tighter beam and virtually nonexistent leakage creates higher signal security. Laser links have a range out to the horizon in clear weather, but range degrades radically in inclement weather. Heavy rain, fog, or smoke renders the system virtually useless.

Satellite uplinks bounce the signal off a communications satellite and down to the master unit. The uplink contains all the software necessary for satellite tracking

and linking. This system provides high signal security and minimal atmospheric interference.

WHITE PHOSPHORUS

White phosphorus is a chemical that burns at very high temperatures when exposed to air. Early smoke grenades spread a curtain of white phosphorus, which created smoke, caused secondary-effect casualties, and ignited combustible materials. Modern (2050) smoke grenades work on the same principle, but burn a less lethal substance to create smoke.

Various suppliers still produce white phosphorus weapons, but their smoke-producing effects are secondary to their incendiary and damage effects. Grenades and mortar rounds designed to deliver white phosphorus have two Damage Codes, the first representing the small blast effect of the actual explosion and the second representing the lingering effect of the white phosphorus. The chemical affects all targets within the area of effect equally. The phosphorous burns continuously for 15 Combat Turns, inflicting the indicated damage every Combat Turn (resolved at the start of each turn during the first Combat Phase). Characters can resist this damage using Body dice only. Impact Armor reduces the Power of the attack. White phosphorus is difficult to extinguish because it re-ignites whenever exposed to air. Water diffuses white phosphorus; if an affected area or target can be immersed or doused with water, the chemical's effects end in 2 Combat Turns.

WEAPON RANGE TABLE

Base Target Number	4	5	6	9
		(Range in Meters)		
Firearms	Short	Medium	Long	Extreme
Hold-out Pistol	0–5	6–15	16–30	31–50
Light Pistol	0–5	6–15	16–30	31–50
Heavy Pistol	0–5	6–20	21–40	41–60
Submachine Gun	0–10	11–40	41–80	81–150
Taser	0–5	6–10	11–12	13–15
Shotgun	0–10	11–20	21–50	51–100
Sport Rifle	0–30	31–60	61–150	151–300
Sniper Rifle	0–40	41–80	81–200	201–400
Assault Rifle	0–15	16–40	41–100	101–250
Light Machine Gun	0–20	21–40	41–80	81–150
Heavy Weapons				
Medium Machine Gun	0–40	41–150	151–300	301–500
Heavy Machine Gun	0–40	41–150	151–400	401–800
Assault Cannon	0–50	51–150	151–450	451–1,300
Grenade Launcher	5–50*	51–100	101–150	151–300
Missile Launcher	20–70*	71–150	151–450	451–1,500
Light Antitank Guided Missile	20–350*	351–750	751–1.5 km	1,50–5 km
Ballista Missile System	20–100*	101–500	501–2,500 m	3,001–5 km
Mortar	150–300*	301 m–1 km	1–4 km	4–6 km
Projectile Weapons				
Bow	0–Str	to Str x 10	to Str x 30	to Str x 60
Light Crossbow	0–Str x 2	to Str x 8	to Str x 20	to Str x 40
Medium Crossbow	0–Str x 3	to Str x 12	to Str x 30	to Str x 50
Heavy Crossbow	0–Str x 5	to Str x 15	to Str x 40	to Str x 60
Throwing Knife	0–Str	to Str x 2	to Str x 3	to Str x 5
Shuriken	0–Str	to Str x 2	to Str x 5	to Str x 7
Grenades				
Standard (1D6 meters Scatter)	0–Str x 3	to Str x 5	to Str x 10	to Str x 20
Aerodynamic (2D6 meters Scatter)	0–Str x 3	to Str x 5	to Str x 20	to Str x 30
Launched (3D6 meters Scatter)	5–50*	51–100	101–150	151–300
Vehicle Weapons				
Vigilant Rotary Autocannon	0–100	101–500	501–2,500	3,001–5 km
Saab Saaker Air-to-Air Missile				
Basic AAM	20 m–700	701–1.5 km	1,501–4.5 km	4,501–15 km
Improved AAM	20 m–15 km	1,501 m–6 km	6,001 m–12 km	12–15 km
Hyundai-CSA Advanced Air-to-Air Missiles				
Basic AAM	20 m–3 km	3,001 m–6 km	6,001 m–12 km	12–15 km
Improved AAM	20 m–5 km	5,001 m–10 km	10–20 km	20–50 km
Ares Dragon's Breath Semi-Smart AAM				
Dogfight AAM	20 m–3 km	3,001 m–6 km	6,001 m–12 km	12–15 km
Attack AAM	20 m–5 km	5,001 m–10 km	10–20 km	20–50 km
Mitsubishi-GM Air-to-Ground Missiles				
Bandit AGM	20–350	351–750	751 m–1.5 km	1,501 m–5 km
Super Bandit AGM	20–700	701 m–1.5 km	1.5–3 km	3–10 km
General Products Unguided Aircraft Rockets				
7.62 cm Rockets	0–150	151–300	301–750	751 m–1.5 km
12.7 cm Rockets	0–300	301–750	751 m–1.5 km	1.5–3 km

*Minimum Range Requirement

The following items have been compiled from the **Shadowrun, Second Edition** rulebook, and the **Street Samurai Catalog (Second Edition), Shadowtech, The Rigger Black Book, Virtual Realities, Shadowbeat, The Grimoire, Second** **Edition**, and **The Neo-Anarchists Guide to Real Life**, as well as this volume, **Fields of Fire**. All notation refers to the **Shadowrun, Second Edition** rules.

WEAPONS

MELEE WEAPONS

	Concealability	Reach	Damage	Weight	Availability	Cost	Street Index
Edged Weapons							
Ares Monosword	3	1	(STR + 3)M	2	4/24 hrs	1,000¥	1
Centurion Laser Axe	2	1	(STR)S	5.2	6/48 hrs	3,500¥	.5
Combat Axe	2	2	(STR)S	2.0	3/24 hrs	750	2
Thrusting Point	NA	0	(STR + 2)L	NA	NA	NA	NA
Survival Knife	6	0	(STR + 2)L	.75	3/6 hrs	450¥	1
Katana	3	1	(STR + 3)M	1	4/48 hrs	1,000¥	2
Knife	8	—	(STR)L	.5	2/4 hrs	30¥	.75
Fineblade Knife (short)	8	—	(STR)M	.5	5/72 hrs	800¥	3
Long Blade	5	—	(STR +1)M	.75	8/72 hrs OK	1,500¥	3
Sword	4	1	(STR + 2)M	1	3/24 hrs	500¥	1
Clubs							
AZ-150 Stun Baton	5	1	8S Stun	1	3/36 hrs	1,500¥	2
Club	5	1	(STR + 1)M Stun	1	2/6 hrs	10¥	1
Sap	8	—	(STR + 2)M Stun	—	2/6 hrs	10¥	1
Stun Baton	4	1	6S Stun	1	3/36 hrs	750¥	1
Pole Arms/Staffs							
Pole Arm	2	2	(STR)S	4	4/48 hrs	500¥	2
Staff	2	2	(STR + 2)M Stun	2	3/24 hrs	50¥	1
Other							
Forearm Snap Blades	7	0	(STR)M	1.5	4/48 hrs	850¥	2
Improved Hand Blades	NA	0	(STR + 2)L	0	6/72 hrs	+8,500¥	1
Monofilament Whip	10	2	10S	—	24/14 days	3,000¥	3
Shock Glove	9	0	7S Stun	.5	5/48 hrs	950¥	2
Unarmed	—	—	(STR)M Stun	—	—	—	—

PROJECTILE WEAPONS

	Concealability	Str. Min	Damage	Weight	Availability	Cost	Street Index
Bows							
Ranger-X Bow	3	2+	(STR + 4)M	1.5	5/36 hrs	120¥ x Str. Min	2
Ranger-X Arrows	4	NA	As bow	.08	4/36 hrs	18¥	1
Standard Bow	2	1+	(STR Min + 2)M	1	3/36 hrs	100¥ x Str. Min.	1
Arrows	3	NA	As bow	.1	3/36 hrs	10¥	1
Crossbows							
Light	2	3	6L	2	4/36 hrs	300¥	1
Medium	2	4	6M	3	5/36 hrs	500¥	1
Heavy	NA	5	8S	4	6/36 hrs	750¥	1
Bolts	4	—	As crossbow	.05	5/36 hrs	5¥	1

THROWING WEAPONS

	Concealability	Str. Min	Damage	Weight	Availability	Cost	Street Index
Non-Aerodynamic							
Throwing Knife	9	NA	(STR)L	.25	2/24 hrs	20¥	1
Aerodynamic							
Shuriken	8	NA	(STR)L	.25	2/24 hrs	30¥	2

FIREARMS

	Conceal	Ammo	Mode	Damage	Weight	Availability	Cost	Street Index
PISTOLS								
Hold-Out								
Morrissey Élan	8	5 (c)	SA	5L	.5	8/7 days	500¥	2
Raecor Sting	9	5 (c)	SS	4M (f)	.25	10/7 days	375¥	2
Streetline Special	8	6 (c)	SS	4L	.5	2/12 hrs	100¥	.75
Tiffani Needler	8	4 (c)	SA	5L	.5	7/48 hrs	650¥	2
Tiffani Self-Defender	8	4 (c)	SS	4L	.5	2/12 hrs	450¥	.75
Walther Palm Pistol	9	2 (b)	SS	4L	.25	3/12 hrs	200¥	.75
Light								
AET NN8	7	12 (c)	SA	6L	1	3/12 hrs	400¥	.8
AET NN8/2	6	25 (c)	SA	6L	1.25	3/12 hrs	450¥	.8
Ares Light Fire 70	5	16 (c)	SA	6L	1	3/12 hrs	475¥	.8
Beretta 200ST	4	26 (c)	SA/BF*	6L	2	5/24 hrs	750¥	1.5
Beretta Model 101T	5	12 (c)	SA	6L	1	3/12 hrs	350¥	.8
Ceska vz/120	7	18 (c)	SA	6L	1	3/12 hrs	500¥	.8
Colt American L36	6	11 (c)	SA	6L	1	3/12 hrs	350¥	.8
Executive Action	6	24 (c)	SA/BF	6L	1.5	14/7 days	1,150¥	3
Fichetti Security 500	7	12 (c)	SA	6L	1	3/12 hrs	400¥	.8
Fichetti Security 500a	6	25 (c)	SA	6L	1.25	3/12 hrs	450¥	.8
Seco LD-120	5	22 (c)	SA	6L	1.25	3/12 hrs	400¥	.8
Walther PB-120	8 (6)	10 (15) (c)	SA	6L	.75	6/36 hrs	700¥	2
Machine Pistols								
Ares Crusader MP	6	40 (c)	SA/BF	6L	3.25	5/36 hrs	950¥	2
Ceska Black Scorpion	5	35 (c)	SA/BF	6L	3	5/36 hrs	850¥	2
Heavy Pistols								
AET NN11	4	25 (c)	SA	9M	2.45	—	Special	—
AET NN12	5	25 (c)	SA/BF	9S(f)	2.2	—	Special	—
AET NN15	8	8 (m)	SA	9S(f)	2.7	—	Special	—
Ares Predator	5	15 (c)	SA	9M	2.25	3/24 hrs	450¥	.5
Ares Predator II	4	15 (c)	SA	9M	2.5	4/24 hrs	550¥	.5
Ares Viper Slivergun	6	30 (c)	SA/BF	9S(f)	2	3/48 hrs	600¥	1
Browning Max-Power	6	10 (c)	SA	9M	2	3/24 hrs	450¥	1
Browning Ultra-Power	6	10 (c)	SA	9M	2.25	4/24 hrs	525¥	1.5
Colt Manhunter	5	16 (c)	SA	9M	2.5	4/24 hrs	425¥	1
Hammerli Model 610S	4	6 (c)	SA	6L	2.5	8/24 hrs	1,295¥	2.5
Morrissey Alta	6	12 (c)	SA	9M	1	8/48 hrs	1,200¥	2
Morrissey Elite	6	5 (c)	SA	9M	1	6/48 hrs	950¥	2
Remington Roomsweeper	8	8 (m)	SA	9S(f)	2.5	3/24 hrs	300¥	1
Ruger Super Warhawk	4	6 (cy)	SS	10M	2.5	3/24 hrs	300¥	1
Savalette Guardian	5	12 (c)	SA/BF	9M	3.25	6/36 hrs	900¥	2.5
SPECIAL WEAPONS								
AET *Dealanach* Taser	4	4 (m)	SA	10S	2	5/24 hrs	1,000¥	1
Bracer	7	1	SS	6L	.3	12/7 days	1,300¥	3
Defiance Super Shock	4	4 (m)	SA	10S	2	5/24 hrs	1,000¥	1
Gun Cane	2/9	1	SS	6L	1	10/7 days *OK*	500¥	2
Narcoject Pistol	7	5 (c)	SA	As toxin	1.5	6/2 days	600¥	2
Naroject Rifle	4	10 (c)	SA	As toxin	3.25	8/2 days *OK*	1,700¥	2
Net Gun, Normal	4	4 (b)	SA	Special	4	8/36 hrs *OK*	750¥	2
Large	3	4 (b)	SA	Special	4.5	8/36 hrs *OK*	1,150¥	2
Yamaha Pulsar (taser)	5	4 (m)	SA	10S Stun	2	12/7 days	1,350¥	2

Toymaker SMG   5 (3)   30 (c)   SA/BF/FA   7M   4   16/7 days   4500   4

Integral SmartLink II. Shock Pads. Imp Gas Vent II. Gyroscopic Stabilization.   Total Recoil Comp: 7

Can be fitted w/ Stock for additional 2 Recoil Comp but -2 Concealability   Capable of 10 rd Full Auto

Cannot Mount Under-Barrel or Barrel

	Conceal	Ammo	Mode	Damage	Weight	Availability	Cost	Street Index
SUBMACHINE GUNS								
AET NN22	4	28 (c)	SA/BF/FA	7M	4	Special	1,500¥	.75
AK-97 SMG/Carbine	4	30 (c)	SA/BF/FA	6M	4	5/3 days	800¥	1
Berretta Model 70	3	35 (c)	BF/FA	6M	3.75	5/3 days	900¥	1
Colt Cobra	5	32 (c)	SA/BF/FA	6M	3	6/36 hrs	700¥	2
Heckler & Koch HK227	4	28 (c)	SA/BF/FA	7M	4	4/24 hrs	1,500¥	.75
Heckler & Koch MP-5TX	5	20 (c)	SA/BF/FA	6M	3.25	5/36 hrs	850¥	1
HK227-S	5	28 (c)	SA/BF	7M	3	10/7 days	1,200¥	2
Ingram Smartgun	5	32 (c)	BF/FA	7M	3	4/24 hrs	950¥	1
Ingram SuperMach 100	5 (4)	40 (60) (c)	SA/BF/FA	6L	3 (3.25)	9/48 hrs	850¥	3
Ingram Warrior-10	4	30 (c)	SA/BF	7M	3	3/24 hrs	650¥	.9
Sandler TMP	4	20 (c)	BF/FA	6M	3.25	5/36 hrs	500¥	1
SCK Model 100	4	30 (c)	SA/BF	7M	4.5	5/36 hrs	1,000¥	1
Steyr AUG-CSL (SMG)*	5	40 (c)	SA/BF	6M	3.5	10/4 days	Special	3
Uzi III	5	24 (c)	BF	6M	2	4/24 hrs	600¥	.75
RIFLES								
Sport Rifles								
Remington 750	3	5 (m)	SA	7S	3	3/24 hrs	600¥	1
Remington 950	2	5 (m)	SA	9S	4	3/24 hrs	800¥	1
Ruger 100	2	5 (m)	SA	7S	3.75	3/24 hrs	1,300¥	1
Steyr AUG-CSL Carbine*	3	40 (c)	SA/BF	7S	3.75	10/4 days	Special	3
Sniper Rifles								
Barret Model 121	—	14 (c)	SA	14D	10	14/30 days	4,800¥	5
Ranger Arms SM-3	—	6 (m)	SA	14S	4	12/7 days OK	4,000¥	4
Walther WA-2100	—	10 (m)	SA	14S	4.5	12/7 days	6,500¥	4
Shotguns								
Defiance T-250	4	5 (m)	SA	10S	3	3/24 hrs	500¥	1
Enfield AS-7	3	10 (c)	SA/BF	8S	4	8/8 days OK	1,000¥	1
Franchi SPAS-22	2 (4)	10 (m)	SA/BF	10S	4	6/48 hrs OK	1,000¥	2
Mossberg SM-CMDT	2	8 (c)	SA/BF	9S	4.5	12/8 days OK	1,900¥	2
Mossberg CMDT	2	8 (c)	SA/BF	9S	4.25	8/8 days OK	1,400¥	1
Remington 990	2	8 (m)	SA	See below*	4	3/48 hrs	650¥	2
Assault Rifles								
Ares Alpha	2	42 (c)	SA/BF/FA	8M	5.25	18/48 hrs	2,000¥	4
Grenade	—	8 (m)	SS	Spec.	—	—	—	—
AK-97	3	38 (c)	SA/BF/FA	8M	4.5	3/36 hrs	700¥	2
AK-98 (w/grenade launcher)	2	38 (c)	SA/BF/FA	8M	6	8/4 days OK	2,500¥	4
Colt M-23	3	40 (c)	SA/BF/FA	8M	4.5	6/36 hrs	950¥	2
Colt M22A2	3	40 (c)	SA/BF/FA	8M	4.75	4/3 days	1,600¥	2
FN HAR	2	35 (c)	SA/BF/FA	8M	4.5	4/48 hrs	1,200¥	2
H&K G12A3z	2	32 (c)	SA/BF/FA	8M	5.25	8/4 days	2,200¥	3
Samopal vz 88V	2	35 (c)	SA/BF/FA	8M	5.5	5/36 hrs	1,800¥	2
Steyr AUG-CSL AR*	2	40 (c)	SA/BF/FA	8M	4	10/4 days	Special	3
LIGHT MACHINE GUNS								
Ares HV MP-LMG	—	80 (c)	SA/BF/FA	6S	8.0	20/14 days	4,500¥	4
Ares MP-LMG	—	Belt 50 (c)	BF/FA	7S	7.5	6/5 days	2,200¥	2
Ingram Valiant	—	Belt 50 (c)	BF/FA	7S	9	6/5 days	1,500¥	2
GE Vindicator Minigun	—	Belt 50 (c)	FA	7S	15	24/14 days	2,500¥	2
Steyr AUG-CSL LMG*	—	40 (c)	SA/BF/FA	8M	5.5	10/4 days	**See note**	3
LASER WEAPONS								
Ares MP Laser	—	20 (Pack)	SA	15M	30	NA	2.5 million¥	NA
Ares MP-Laser III	—	20 (Pack)	SA	15M	25	24/21 days	120,000¥	3

HEAVY WEAPONS	Conceal	Ammo	Mode	Damage	Weight	Availability	Cost	Street Index
FN MAG-5 MMG	—	Belt 50 (Box)	FA	9S	9.5	18/14 days	3,200¥	3
Generic Assault Cannon	—	20 (c)	SS	18D	20	16/14 days	6,500¥	2
Generic HMG	—	40 (c)	FA	10S	15	18/18 days	4,000¥	2
Generic MMG	—	40 (c)	FA	9S	12	14/14 days	2,500¥	2
Stoner-Ares M107 HMG	—	Belt 50 (Box)	FA	10S	12.5	18/14 days	5,200¥	3
Panther Assault Cannon	—	22 (c) Belt	SS	18D	18	16/14 days	7,200¥	2
GRENADE LAUNCHERS								
Generic Under-Barrel	(–3)	6 (m)	SS	grenade	+2 kg	8/4 days *OK*	1,700¥	3
MGL-12	3	12 (c)	SA	Variable*	5.0	6/36 hrs	2,200¥	3
MGL-6	6	6 (c)	SA	Variable*	2.5	6/36 hrs	1,600¥	3
MISSLE/ROCKET LAUNCHER								
Multi-Launcher	—	4 (b)	SS	—	8	12/14 days	8,000¥	2
ROCKET LAUNCHERS								
M79B1 LAW	4/—*	1	SS	12D	2.5	6/36 hrs	700¥	2
Arbelast II MAW	—	1	SS	15D	2.75	8/48 hrs	1,200¥	2

MISSILE LAUNCHERS

	Type	Intelligence	Ammo	Mode	Damage	Weight	Availability	Cost	Street Index
Great Dragon	L-ATGM	4	1	SS	20D	2.75	8/48 hrs	1,200¥	2
Ballista Missile Launcher	Missile	—	4 (m)	SS	14D	6.5	18/30 days	10,500¥	4

MORTARS

	Conceal	Ammo	Mode	Damage	Weight	Availability	Cost	Street Index
M-12 Portable	—	1	SS	Special	30	12/14 days	3,000¥	2

AMMUNITION

ROCKET/MISSILES

ROCKETS	Intelligence	Damage	Weight	Availability	Cost	Street Index
Anti-Personnel	NA	16D	2	8/14 days	1,000¥	2
Anti-Vehicle	NA	16D	3	8/14 days	2,000¥	2
High-Explosive	NA	16D	2	8/14 days	1,500¥	2
Missiles						
Anti-Personnel	3	16D	2.25	12/14 days	2,500¥	3
Anti-Vehicle	4	16D	3.25	12/14 days	5,000¥	3
High-Explosive	3	16D	2.25	12/14 days	3,750¥	3
Surface to Air (SAM)	4	13 D	1.5	18/21 days	2,500¥	4

BALLISTA ROCKET AND MISSILE ROUNDS

	Intelligence	Damage	Blast	Weight	Cost	Availability	Street Index
Mk I	0	14D	–7/meter	2.75	1,000¥	12/21 days	4
Mk II	5*	14D	–7/meter	2.75	2,000¥	18/28 days	4
Mk III	6	14 D	–7/meter	2.75	2,500¥	14/28 days	4

MORTAR ROUNDS

	Damage	Blast	Weight	Cost	Availability	Street Index
High Explosive	18D	–1/ .5m	4.0	200¥	18/14 days	3
Anti-Personnel*	18D	–1/ 1m	4.0	250¥	18/14 days	3
Smoke**	—	—	3.5	175¥	14 days	2
White Phosphorus†	15S/12L	–1/ 1m	4.0	350¥	18/14 days	3
Anti-Vehicle††	16D	–1/ 4m	4.0	1,200¥	21 days	4

Shredders 8 +1 Staging .25 9/72 hrs 250 3 vs Double Impact

Explosive APDS 8 +2 Power / vs ½ Ballistic .5 20/14 days 150 5 vs ½ Ballistic

TABLES

AMMUNITION, PER 10 SHOTS

	Concealability*	Damage	Weight	Availability**	Cost	Street Index	
APDS	8	See rules	.25	14/14 days	70¥	4	vs ½ Ballistic
Assault Cannon	3	As weapon	1.25	5/3 days	450¥	2	
Belt 100	yeah, right	—	12.5	6/3 days	4,250¥	2	
Explosive Rounds	8	See rules +1 Power	.75	3/36 hrs	50¥	.8	
EX Explosive	8	See rules +2 Power	.75	6/72 hrs	100¥	1.5	
Flechette Rounds	8	See rules +1 Staging	.5	3/36 hrs	100¥	.8	vs Double Impact or Ballistic
Gel Rounds	8	See rules -2 Power	.25	4/48 hrs	30¥	1	vs Impact Armor
Regular Ammo	8	As weapon	.5	2/24 hrs	20¥	.75	
Stun Rounds	8	See rules	1	4/48 hrs	100¥	1	
Tracer / Neurostun	8/6	See rules	.5/.75	3/24 hrs 6/36 hrs	75¥/1000¥	1/2	
Taser Dart / Shock Battery	3/8	Special	.5	6/36 hrs	50¥/100¥	1.5	vs ½ Impact

*−1 Concealability per extra 10 rounds of ammo

**Belted ammo: add rounds/100 to Availability

AP Rounds 8 vs Impact +1 Power −1 Staging .5 4/48 hrs 190¥ .8

FIREARM AND WEAPON ACCESSORIES

	Mount	Concealability	Rating	Weight	Availability	Cost	Street Index
GENERAL							
Bipod	Under	—	—	2	6/12 hrs	400¥	1
Bow Accessory Mount	NA	−1	—	.1	2/24 hrs	100¥	.9
Concealable Holster	—	+2	—	.1	2/24 hrs	100¥	.75
Rangefinder	Under/Top	—	—	.1	2/24 hrs	150¥	.8
Grenade Link	—	—	—	.1	8/48 hrs	750¥	2
Silencer	Barrel	−2	—	.2	4/48 hrs	500¥	2
Sound Suppresser	Barrel	−2	—	.5	6/48 hrs	750¥	2
Spare Clips	—	—	—	.75	2/24 hrs	5¥	.75
Tripod	Under	—	6	8	10/12 hrs	600¥	1
RECOIL COMPENSATORS AND GYROS							
Deluxe Imp. Gyro Mount	Under	−7	7	7	6/48 hrs	7,800¥	1
Gas Vent II	Barrel	−1	1	.5	2/24 hrs	450¥	.8
Gas Vent III	Barrel	−2	2	.75	2/24 hrs	700¥	1
Gyro Mount, Deluxe	—	−6	6	8	4/48 hrs	6,000¥	1
Gyro Mount, Standard	—	−5	5	6	4/48 hrs	2,500¥	1
Imp. Gas Vent II	Barrel	—	2	.25	2/24 hrs	550¥	.9
Imp. Gas Vent III	Barrel	−1	3	.5	2/24 hrs	800¥	.9
Imp. Gas Vent IV	Barrel	−2	4	.75	2/24 hrs	1,000¥	1
Imp. Gyro Mount	Under	−6	5	5	6/48 hrs	3,500¥	1
Shock Pads	—	—	1	.25	2/24 hrs	200¥	.75
IMAGING SYSTEMS							
Imaging Scopes							
Low-Light	Top	−2	—	.25	3/36 hrs	1,500¥	.8
Magnification 1	Top	−1	1	.25	3/36 hrs	500¥	.8
Magnification 2	Top	−1	2	.25	3/36 hrs	800¥	.9
Magnification 3	Top	−1	3	.25	3/36 hrs	1,200¥	1
Thermographic	Top	−2	—	.25	3/36 hrs	1,500¥	.8
Laser Sights	Top	−1	—	.25	6/36 hrs	500¥	.9
Ultrasound Sight	Top	−2	—	.25	8/4 days	1,300¥	.8
Ultrasound Goggles	NA	—	—	—	3/36 hrs	1,100¥	1
SMARTLINK (LEVEL I)							
Smart Goggles	—	0	—	.1	3/36 hrs	3,000¥	1
Smartgun, internal	—	—	—	.5	Weapon	+100%	Weapon
Smartgun, external	Top/under	−2	—	1	4/48 hrs	600¥	1
SMARTLINK (LEVEL II)							
Smartgoggles	—	0	—	.1	4/36 hrs	3,500¥	2
External Smartgun	Top/under	−2	—	75	6/48 hrs	800¥	2
Internal Smartgun	—	—	—	.25	Weapon	+250%	Weapon

TARGET DESIGNATORS

	Conceal	Range	Weight	Availability	Cost	Street Index
Low-power laser sight	−1	500m	.25	6/36 hrs	500¥	.9
High-power laser sight	−1	1,500m	.25	8/48 hrs	1,400¥	1
Laser designator	−2	5,000m	.5	12/14 days	3,700¥	2
Microwave designator	—	8,000 km	4.5	24/1 mth	12,500¥	2
Radar designator	—	10,000 km+	25	24/3 mths	48,000¥	2

EXPLOSIVES

GRENADES

Grenade Type	Conceal	Damage	Weight	Availability	Cost	Street Index
Offensive (HE* or AP)	6	10S (−1/ meter)	.25	4 days	30¥	2
IPE Offensive (HE* or AP)	6	15S (−1/meter)	.25	5/4 days	50¥	2
Defensive (HE* or AP)	6	10S (−1/ .5 meter)	.25	4 days	30¥	2
IPE Defensive (HE* or AP)	6	15S (−1/ .5 meter)	.25	5/4 days	50¥	2
Concussion	6	12M (Stun) (−1/ meter)	.25	5/4 days	30¥	2
IPE Concussion	6	16M (Stun) (−1/meter)	.25	5/4 days	70¥	2
White Phosphorus	6	14M/10L (−1/meter)	.25	6/5 days	120¥	3
Smoke†	6	—	.25	3/24 hrs	30¥	2
Smoke (IR)	6	—	.25	4/48 hrs	40¥	2
Flash	6	Special	.25	4/48 hrs	40¥	1
Mini-grenade	8	by grenade	.1	+2/by grenade	x2	+1
Air Timed Mini-Grenade	8	by grenade	.1	+3/by grenade	x4	+2

COMMERCIAL EXPLOSIVES, PER KILO

w/ Grenade Link, −1 Scatter

	Concealability	Rating	Weight	Availability	Cost	Street Index
Commercial	6	3	1	6/48 hrs	60¥	1
Plastic, Compound IV	6	6	1	8/48 hrs	80¥	1
Plastic, Compound XII	6	12	1	10/48 hrs	200¥	2
Accessories						
Radio Detonator	8	—	.25	4/48 hrs	250¥	2
Timer	6	—	.5	4/48 hrs	100¥	2

CLOTHING AND ARMOR

	Concealability	Ballistic	Impact	Weight	Availability	Cost	Street Index
GENERAL							
Fine Clothing	—	0	0	1	Always	500¥	1
Forearm Guards	12	0	1	.2	5/36 hrs	250¥	.75
Ordinary Clothing	—	0	0	1	Always	50¥	.8
Riot Shield, Small	—	1		2	8/14 days	1,500¥	2
Tres Chic	—	0	0	1	Always	1,000¥	1
ARMOR CLOTHING							
Armor Clothing	10	3	0	2	2/36 hrs	500¥	1
Armor Jacket	6	5	3	2	3/36 hrs	900¥	.75
Armor Vest	12	2	1	1	2/36 hrs	200¥	.8
Lined Coat	8	4	2	1	2/24 hrs	700¥	.75
Secure Clothing	12	3	0	1.5	3/36 hrs	450¥	.9
Secure Jacket	9	5	3	3	4/36 hrs	850¥	.8
Secure Vest	15	2	1	.75	3/36 hrs	175¥	.9
Secure Ultra-Vest	14	4	3	2.5	3/36 hrs	350¥	.9
Secure Long Coat	10	4	2	2	3/24 hrs	650¥	.9
Vest with Plates	10	4	3	2	3/36 hrs	600¥	1
Armanté							
"Venetian" dress	14	1	0	.5	2/48 hrs	3,500¥	.75
"Starlight" dress	13	1	1	.75	2/48 hrs	4,500¥	.75

	Concealability	Ballistic	Impact	Weight	Availability	Cost	Street Index
"*Ancien*" shawl	14	1	0	.3	2/48 hrs	750¥	.75
"Executive Suite" tux	12	3	1	1	4/48 hrs	1,100¥	.75
"London Fog" cloak	12	2	2	1	4/48hrs	600¥	.75
Mortimer of London							
"Greatcoat"	11	4	2	3	6/48 hrs	1,000¥	.75
Vashon Island							
"Houndstooth" suit jacket	14	1.5	.5	1		See Package Cost	
"Houndstooth" pants	14	1	.5	1		See Package Cost	
"Houndstooth" suit vest	13	.5	1	.75		See Package Cost	
"Houndstooth" sprt. jckt.	12	.5	1.5	1.25		See Package Cost	
"Houndstooth" package	—	—	—	—	7/48 hrs	2,000¥	.75
"Hunts Ball" jacket	13	.5	1.5	1.25		See Package Cost	
"Hunts Ball" skirt	14	.5	1	1		See Package Cost	
"Hunts Ball" slacks	14	1	.5	1		See Package Cost	
"Hunts Ball" package	—	—	—	—	5/48 hrs	3,000¥	.75
Zoé							
"Retrovision" skirt suit	13	3	1	1.5	4/48 hrs	2,500¥	.75
"Country Club" blazer	13	3	1	1	4/48 hrs	2,000¥	.75
"Highland Laird" kilt	14	4	2	1.5	6/48 hrs	2,000¥	.75
CAMOUFLAGE							
Camo Full Suit	—	3	1	1.5	4/36 hrs	800¥	1
Camo Jacket	—	5	3	2	5/36 hrs	1,200¥	1
FORM-FITTING BODY ARMOR							
Level 1	—	2	0	.75	3/48 hrs	150¥	1
Level 2	15	3	1	1.25	4/48 hrs	250¥	1
Level 3	12	4	1	1.75	4/48 hrs	500¥	1
LEATHER							
Real	—	0	2	1	Always	750¥	.75
Synthetic	—	0	1	1	Always	250¥	.6
HEAVY ARMOR							
Partial Suit	—	6	4	10 + Body	8/10 days	10,000¥	2
Full Suit	—	8	6	15 + Body	16/14 days	20,000¥	3
Helmet	—	+1	1+	— 1	12/14 days	200¥	1.5
MILITARY GRADE ARMOR							
Light Military Armor	—	10	7	12 + Body	18/1 mth	25,000¥	3
Medium Military Armor	—	12	8	14 + Body	24/1 mth	45,000¥	3
Heavy Military Armor	—	14	9	16 + Body	28/1.5 mths	70,000¥	3
Heavy Military Helmet	—	+2	+3	3.0	24/1 mth	2,500¥	3
SECURITY ARMOR							
Light Security	—	6	4	9 + Body	12/10 days	7,500¥	2
Medium Security	—	6	5	11 + Body	14/10 days	9,000¥	2.5
Heavy Security	—	7	5	13 + Body	16/14 days	12,000¥	3
Security Helmet	—	+1	+2	— 2	12/14 days	250¥	2

LIFESTYLE

ENTERTAINMENT

	Concealability	Weight	Availability	Cost	Street Index
Music					
Disk/Chip	8	—	Always	20¥	.75
Playback Unit	3	2	Always	200¥	.75
Quad Speakers	—	—	Always	100¥	.75
Video					
Disk/Chip	8	—	Always	20¥	.75
Recorder Package	2	2	6/48 hrs	1,000¥	1.5
Screen	—	3	Always	150¥	.75
Transmission Unit	—	5	8/7 days	4,000¥	2

Simsense Decks	Concealability	Weight	Availability	Cost	Street Index
Truman Dreambox (monoPOV ACT)	3	3	Always	350¥	.75
Sony Beautiful Dreamer (monoPOV ACT)	3	3	Always	200¥	1
Sony Beautiful Dreamer II (polyPOV ACT)	2	5	Always	1,800¥	1
Fuchi Dreamliner (polyPOV ACT)	2	5.5	Always	2,500¥	1
Truman Paradiso (polyPOV ACT and DIR-X)	—	6	4/36 hrs	75,000¥	1
Fuchi RealSense™ MasterSim (Commercial Dir-X)	—	12	8/1 week	125,000¥	3
ASIST Dir-X Multiplexer	—	7	8/1 week	2,500¥ + (100¥ per channel)	3

Simsense Recordings

(All prices shown are for baseline recordings. Triple prices for full-X. Concealability is 10, Availability is Always. Street Index is .75)

	Cost
ACT Recordings	
Cheap or Instructional Recording	1¥/minute
Average Entertainment or Documentary	2¥/minute
High-Quality Entertainment or Documentary	2.5¥/minute
Current Hit	3¥/minute
Dir-X Recordings	
Average Entertainment or Documentary	90¥/minute
High-Quality Entertainment or Documentary	100¥/minute
Current Hit	150¥/minute

ELECTRONICS

	Concealability	Weight	Availability	Cost	Street Index
Telecom	—	15	Always	Memory Cost x 1.5	1
PORTABLE PHONES					
Wrist Models	4	—	Always	1,000¥	.75
With Flip-Up Screen	—	—	Always	1,500¥	1
Handset Unit	3	1	Always	500¥	.75
Earplug Unit	8	—	Always	1,000¥	1.5
Booster Pack	3	2	Always	500¥	1
Pocket Secretary	3	.5	Always	3,000¥	1
PERSONAL COMPUTERS					
Table Top	—	10	Always	Memory Cost	.75
Pocket	3	1	Always	Memory Cost x 5	1
Wrist	4	—	Always	Memory Cost x 20	1.5
Printer	NA	10	Always	100¥	1
Computer Memory (Non-Cyber)	NA	—	Always	20¥ x Mp	.75
DATA DISPLAY SYSTEMS (w/max memory capacity)					
Data Unit (1,000 Mp)	3	2	Always	Memory Cost	1
Headset (500 Mp)	4	1	Always	Memory Cost x 2	1.5
Heads-Up Display (200 Mp)	NA	1	6/7 days	Memory Cost x 10	3

WORKING GEAR

	Concealability	Weight	Availability	Cost*	Street Index
Kit	3	5	5/48 hrs	500¥	2
Shop	—	—	8/72 hrs	5,000¥	3
Facility	—	—	14/7 days	100,000¥	4

*General Work (Base Cost). Vehicle Work (2 x Cost). Electronic/Computer/Cyberware Work (3 x Cost).

MEDIA EQUIPMENT

	Concealability	Weight	Availability	Cost	Street Index
PORTACAMS AND CYBERCAMS					
Fuchi VX2200 Portacam	—	3	2/48 hrs	1,000¥	1
Fuchi VX2200C Cybercam	—	5	3/48 hrs	1,300¥	2
Sony HB500 Portacam	—	3.5	4/72 hrs	2,200¥	2
Sony CB5000 Cybercam	—	5.5	5/72 hrs	2,700¥	2
AZT Micro20 Microportacam	8	2.5	5/72 hrs	2,500¥	2
AZT Micro25 Microcybercam	8	2.5	5/72 hrs	3,200¥	2
Bionome Tridlink Adapter	6	1	2/72 hrs	700¥	1
PORTACAM BASES					
Kodak GAC-25 Shoulder Mount	—	1	3/48 hrs	200¥	2
Cinema Products Steadicam™					
Shoulder	—	2	3/48 hrs	1,800¥	2
Chest	—	3	3/48 hrs	1,800¥	2
Head	—	2	3/48 hrs	1,800¥	2
AZT Micro30 StaticBrace					
(for the Micro20 Portacam Series)					
Wrist	—	1	3/48 hrs	2,200¥	1
Chest	—	2	3/48 hrs	2,200¥	1
CAMGOGGLES					
Fuchi I-C-U Autocam Controller	5	1.5	5/72 hrs	400¥	2
Zeemandt Luxor Monocular	6	.5	5/72 hrs	700¥	2
Sekrit Sistemz No-Sho Camtroller	5	1	5/72 hrs	1,000¥	2
Smartcam Adapter	N/A	.5	5/72 hrs	1,500¥	2
TRANSMITTER LINKS					
Unsecured Transmitter Links					
Short-haul	6	5	4/72 hrs	4,000¥	2
Long-haul	4	4	4/72 hrs	6,000¥	2
Uplink	2	3	4/72 hrs	1,000¥	2
Secured Transmitter Links					
Short-haul	4	5	5/72 hrs	6,000¥	3
Long-haul	2	4	5/72 hrs	9,000¥	3
Uplink	—	3	5/72 hrs	1,500¥	3
TRIDISYNTHS AND MIXERS					
Vertex Netsynth Tridmixer	—	7	2/48 hrs	8,000¥	1
Fuchi Holo-Edit 7200	—	9	4/72 hrs	10,000¥	2
Sony TFX-10000 Imaging Generator	—	7	8/1 week	13,000¥	2
PIRATE EQUIPMENT					
Electromagnetic Transmitters (Radio/TV/3V)					
Non-mobile	—	35	8/1 week	5,500¥	1
Mobile	—	25	8/2 weeks	7,500¥	2
+ECM Rating (1 to 6)	—	—	+1/point	+2,500¥/rating point	3
Transmission Sampler	6	5	8/1 week	1,000¥	2
Satellite Injection Uplink Station	—	20	8/2 weeks	1,000¥	2
+ECM Rating (1 to 6)	—	—	+1/point	+3,000¥/rating point	3
Cable Signal Formatter	3	3	8/1 week	2,000¥	2
+ECM Rating (1 to 6)	—	—	+1/point	+1,500¥/rating point	3

PROGRAMMABLE ASIST BIOFEEDBACK

	Concealablity	Weight	Availability	Cost	Street Index
Galil Ruach-Aleph Reprogrammer	3	2	8/1 week	10,000¥	3
Mitsuhama MenTokko-II Engram Manipulator	4	3	8/2 weeks	15,000¥	3
Ares CyberMed Psychscanner	—	10	8/2 weeks	25,000¥	3
EBMM Therapeutic ASIST System	—	12	8/2 weeks	40,000¥	3
Mitsuhama MenTokko-V Engram Manipulator	—	14	12/3 weeks	60,000¥	3

	Concealablity	Weight	Availability	Cost	Street Index
SIMSENSE GEAR					
Simlinks					
External (Rating 1-10)	8	.5	8/2 weeks	25,000¥ + (5k¥ x Rating)	2
Simths					
Truman Reality-500 (monoPOV Baseline)	—	15	8/1 week	25,000¥	2
Fuchi RealSense™ Kosmos XXV	—	30	8/2 week	250,000¥	3
Truman Inner-I	—	28	8/2 week	200,000¥	3
Simth Peripherals					
ASIST Enablers:					
EC/PC Enabler	5	6	8/1 week	Rating x 10,000¥	2
Emotive Enabler	2	7	8/1 week	Rating x 25,000¥	2
Sense Patch Injector	4	5	8/1 week	25,000¥	2
Signal Peak Controller	4	5.5	8/1 week	15,000¥	2
Experience Samplers					
MonoPOV ACT Format	—	13	8/1 week	15,000¥	2
MonoPOV Dir-X Format	—	14	8/1 week	75,000¥	2
PolyPOV Samplers	—	10	—	+25% per additional POV	—

MUSICAL INSTRUMENTS

(None of the below are Concealable. Availability is Always. Street Index is 8.)

Quality	Common*	Rare*
Cheap	50¥	250¥
Average	500¥	2,500¥
Fine	5,000¥	25,000¥

*Actual price = Basic Price x Complexity. Electric instruments and synthesizer controllers reduce Complexity by 1(see p. 92, **Shadowbeat**).

Synthesizers	Cost
Cheap (max 8 voices)	150¥ + 25¥ per voice.
Average (max 16 voices)	500¥ + 100¥ per voice.
Fine (max 32 voices)	5,000¥ + 500¥ per voice.
Autosynths	
Skill 1–3	1,000¥ per skill point
Skill 4–5	3,000¥ per skill point
Skill 6–8	5,000¥ per skill point
Skill 9–10	10,000¥ per skill point

Synthlink Equipment

	Concealability	Weight	Availability	Cost	Street Index
Synthlink Controller					
Cheap	6	.5	Always	1,000¥	.75
Average	5	.5	Always	10,000¥	.75
Fine	5	.5	3/48 hrs	50,000¥	1

SOUND SYSTEM COMPONENTS

(None of the below are Concealable. Availability is Always. Street Index is 8.)

	Cost
Acoustic Modulators	
Small	8,000¥
Club	15,000¥
Hall	35,000¥
Amplifiers	
Small	100¥
Club	400¥
Hall	1,200¥
Stadium	5,000¥
Superstadium	12,000¥
Speakers	
Small	100¥
Club	1,000¥

	Cost
Hall	5,000¥
Stadium	12,000¥
Superstadium	25,000¥
Direct Digital Output	
Built-in DDO	+500¥ to base price
DDO Adapter	+700¥ to base price
Multitrack Samplers	
4-track Sampler	1,200¥
8-track Sampler	3,200¥
16-track Sampler	8,000¥
24-track Sampler	14,400¥
32-track Sampler	22,400¥
Manual Control Only	Base Price
Direct Neural Interface Control Only	Base Price x 2
Combined Manual/DNI Control	Base Price x 2.5

	Concealability	Weight	Availability	Cost	Street Index
Microphones					
Body Mike	10	.1	2/36 hrs	100¥	1
Hand Mike	6	.5	Always	100¥	1
Mike Stand	—	3	Always	50¥	1
Mike Boom	—	3	3/36 hrs	75¥	2
Mixers					
Basic unit	8	2	Always	1,000¥	1
Per additional input channel	NA	NA	3/36 hrs	+200¥	2
Per additional output channel	NA	NA	NA	+500¥	2
Built-in Polycorder	NA	NA	5/36 hrs	+300¥	2
Polycorders					
Microcorder (3 x 3 x 1 cm)	8	—	6/48 hrs	1,000¥	2
Minicorder (5 x 3 x 1 cm)	6	.1	4/24 hrs	700¥	1
Pocket sized (10 x 5 x 3 cm)	5	.2	Always	200¥	.75
Hand-held (20 x 8 x 4 cm)	2	2.5	Always	100¥	.75
Rack-mount Component	—	4	3/24 hrs	1,500¥	2
Sprawl Blaster (built-in small speakers)	—	3.5	Always	200¥	.75
Sprawl Fuserr (built-in club speakers)	—	5.5	Always	1,200¥	.75
MiniCD Transport Only	—	—	—	Base Price/2	.75
ASIST Direct Neural Playback	—	—	—	Base Price x 3	2

SURVEILLANCE AND SECURITY

VISION ENHANCERS

	Concealability	Magnification	Weight	Availability	Cost	Street Index
Binoculars	5	50x	1	Always	100¥	.8
Low-Light	—	—	—	4/48 hrs	+200¥	1.25
Thermographic	—	—	—	4/48 hrs	+250¥	1.25
Goggles	6	20x	—	4/48 hrs	1,500¥	1.5
Low-Light	—	—	—	6/48 hrs	+500¥	2
Thermographic	—	—	—	6/48 hrs	+700¥	2

Semi Cyber Vision   15 000

COMMUNICATIONS

	Concealability	Weight	Availability	Cost	Street Index
Micro-Camcorder	8	—	6/48 hrs	2,500¥	2
Micro-Recorder	9	—	6/48 hrs	1,000¥	2
Micro-Transceiver	18	—	6/48 hrs	2,500¥	2

TABLES

TACTICAL COMMUNICATION SYSTEM

	Concealability	Rating	Weight	Availability	Cost	Street Index
Master Unit	—	14	75	24/21 days	60,000¥	3
Portable Master Unit	—	14	20	18/14 days	120,000¥	2
Personal Comm Unit	8	14	.5	12/14 days	18,500¥	2
Microwave Link	3	—	1.0	18/21 days	4,800¥	2
Laser Link	4	—	1.0	14/21 days	2,700¥	2
Satellite Uplink	—	—	2.0	12/21 days	7,500¥	2

SURVEILLANCE MEASURES

	Concealability	Weight	Availability	Cost	Street Index
Data Codebreaker	2	5	Rating/10 days	10,000¥ x Rating	1.5
Dataline Tap	12	—	Rating/8 days	5,000¥ x Rating	1.5
Laser Microphone	5	1	Rating/48 hrs	1,500¥ x Rating	1.5
Shotgun Microphone	5	1	Rating/36 hrs	1,000¥ x Rating	1
Signal Locator	3	2	Rating/48 hrs	1,000¥ x Rating	1.5
Tracking Signal	3	—	Rating/72 hrs	100¥ x Concealability	2
Voice Identifier	2	5	Rating/72 hrs	2,000¥ x Rating	2

SURVEILLANCE COUNTERMEASURES

	Concealability	Weight	Availability	Cost	Street Index
Bug Scanner	3	1	Rating/48 hrs	500¥ x Rating	1.5
Data Encryption System	2	6	Rating/14 days	1,000¥ x Rating	2
Dataline Scanner	2	6	Rating/14 days	100¥ x Rating	2
Jammer	2	5	Rating / 72 hrs	1,000¥ x Rating	1.5
Voice Mask	6	—	Rating/72 hrs	3,000¥ x Rating	1.5
White Noise Generator	3	1	Rating/72 hrs	1,500¥ x Rating	1.5

SECURITY DEVICES

	Concealability	Weight	Availability	Cost	Street Index
Identification Scanners					
Thumbprint	—	—	Rating/72 hrs	200¥ x Rating	1
Palmprint	—	—	(Rating + 1)/72 hrs	300¥ x Rating	2
Retinal	—	—	(Rating + 2)/72 hrs	1,000¥ x Rating	3
Maglocks	—	—	Rating/72 hrs	100¥ x Rating	1
PANICBUTTON Hook-Up	—	—	Call Lone Star	1,000¥	1
Maglock Passkey (illegal)	—	1	(Rating x 2)/10 days	10,000¥ x Rating	3
Restraints					
Metal	3	.5	4/48 hrs	50¥	1
Plastic	3	—	4/48 hrs	20¥	1
Squealer	4	—	6/72 hrs	100¥	2

SURVIVAL GEAR

	Concealability	Weight	Availability	Cost	Street Index
Chemsuit	—	1	(Rating/Rating) days	200¥ x Rating	1
Pressure Regulator	—	.5	6/48 hrs	250¥	2
Ration Bars (10 Days)	—	1	2/48 hrs	30¥	1
Respirator	—	1	4/48 hrs	500¥	2
Survival Kit	—	2	2/48 hrs	100¥	1

CLIMBING GEAR

	Weight	Availability	Cost	Street Index
Ascent/Descent Harness	.25	Always	75¥	1
Ascent/Descent Kit*	2.0	Always	250¥	1
Rappelling Gloves	—	Always	70¥	1
Rope (50m)	1.0	Always	125¥	1

GLOBAL POSITIONING SYSTEM

	Concealability	Weight	Availability	Cost	Street Index
Nav-Dat™	8	.5	6/48 hrs	700¥	1

CYBERTECH

HEADWARE

	Essence Cost	Cost	Availability	Street Index
Chemical Analyzer	.2	2,500¥/Level	4/6 days	1
Chipjack	.2	1,000¥	3/72 hrs	.9
Cortex Bomb (illegal)	—	500,000¥	20/14 days	1
Data Filter	.3	5,000¥	6/36 hrs	1.5
Datajack (**SR** rules)	.2	1,000¥	Always	.9
Datajack (**Shadowtech**)				
Level 1	.1	500¥	Always	.9
Level 2	.15	1,000¥	Always	.9
Level 3	.2	2,000¥	Always	.9
Level 4	.25	4,000¥	Always	.9
Data Lock	.2	1,000¥	6/36 hrs	1.5
Datasoft Link	.1	1,000¥	3/24 hrs	1
Encephalon				
Level 1	.5	15,000¥	6/12 days	2
Level 2	.75	40,000¥	6/12 days	2
Level 3	1.5	75,000¥	6/12 days	2
Level 4	1.75	115,000¥	6/12 days	2
Gas Spectrometer	.2	2,000¥/Level	4/5 days	1
Internal Voice Mask	.1	7,000¥	6/48 hrs	1
Memory	Mp ÷ 100	Mp x 100¥	2/24 hrs	1
Memory (FIFF)	Mp/300	Mp x 150¥	3/24 hrs	.8
Olfactory Booster	.2	1,000¥/Level	6/8 days	1
Orientation System	.5	15,000¥	5/6 days	1.5
Sense Link	2	300,000¥	2/5 days	1
Internal Transmitter	.6	80,000¥	3/5 days	1.5
Softlink (Level 1)	.15	1,000Y	3/72 hrs	.9
Level 2	.2	2,000¥	3/72 hrs	.9
Level 3	.25	4,000¥	3/72 hrs	.9
Level 4	.3	8,000¥	3/72 hrs	.9
SPU: Data Management				
Level 1	.1	9,500¥	6/60 hrs	1
Level 2	.15	19,000¥	6/60 hrs	1
Level 3	.2	28,500¥	6/60 hrs	1
Level 4	.25	38,000¥	6/60 hrs	1
SPU: Input/Output				
Level 1	.1	5,000¥	5/4 days	1.5
Level 2	.15	7,500¥	5/4 days	1.5
Level 3	.2	12,500¥	5/4 days	1.5
Level 4	.25	22,500¥	5/4 days	1.5
SPU: Math				
Level 1	.1	2,000¥	6/60 hrs	1
Level 2	.15	5,000¥	6/60 hrs	1
Level 3	.2	11,000¥	6/60 hrs	1
Level 4	.25	23,000¥	6/60 hrs	1
Tactical Computer				
Level 1	3.5	350,000¥	12/60 days	4
Level 2	4	900,000¥	12/60 days	4
Level 3-4	**CLASSIFIED**		**CLASSIFIED**	

	Essence Cost	Cost	Availability	Street Index
Video Link	.5	22,000¥	4/48 hrs	1
Internal Transmitter	.4	4,500¥	6/48 hrs	1
Communications				
Commlink II	.3	8,000¥	2/48 hrs	1
Commlink IV	.3	18,000¥	3/48 hrs	1.25
Commlink VIII	.3	40,000¥	4/48 hrs	1.5
Commlink X	.3	60,000¥	5/48 hrs	1.75
Crypto Circuit HD				
Level 1–4	.1	Level x 10,000¥	6/36 hrs	1
Level 5–7	.1	Level x 20,000¥	6/36 hrs	1.25
Level 8–9	.1	Level x 30,000¥	8/36 hrs	1.5
Level 10	.1	500,000¥	9/36 hrs	2
Radio	.75	4,000¥	2/24 hrs	.8
Radio Receiver	.4	2,000¥	2/24 hrs	.8
Scramble Breaker HD				
Level 1–4	.2	Level x 20,000¥	6/48 hrs	1.5
Level 5–7	.2	Level x 40,000¥	8/48 hrs	1.75
Level 10	.2	600,000¥	10/48 hrs	1.75
Telephone	.5	3,700¥	3/24 hrs	.9
Ears				
Cosmetic Modification	—	1,000¥	2/24 hrs	.8
Cyber Replacement	.2	4,000¥	2/24 hrs	.75
Damper	.1	3,500¥	4/48 hrs	1.25
Hearing Amplification	.2	3,500¥	4/48 hrs	1.25
High Frequency	.2	3,000¥	4/48 hrs	1.25
Low Frequency	.2	3,000¥	4/48 hrs	1.25
Modification	.1	2,000¥	2/24 hrs	1
Recorder	.3	7,000¥	8/48 hrs	2
Select Sound Filter (Levels 1–5)	.2	Level x 10,000¥	6/48 hrs	1.25
Eyes				
Camera	.4	5,000¥	6/24 hrs	2
Cosmetic Modification	—	1,000¥	2/24 hrs	.75
Cyber Replacement	.2	5,000¥	2/24 hrs	.75
Display Link	.1	1,000¥	4/36 hrs	1
Dr. Spott Smartcam Implant	2	10,000¥	6/4 days	2
Eyecrafters Opticam Package	.5	20,000¥	5/72 hrs	2
Flare Compensation	.1	2,000¥	5/48 hrs	1.25
Low-Light	.2	3,000¥	4/36 hrs	1.25
Rangefinder	.1	2,000¥	8/48 hrs	1.5
Retinal Duplication (illegal)	.1	50,000¥+	12/7 days	2
Thermographic	.2	3,000¥	4/36 hrs	1.25
Vision Magnification				
Optical 1	.2	2,500¥	4/48 hrs	1
Optical 2	.2	4,000¥	4/48 hrs	1
Optical 3	.2	6,000¥	5/48 hrs	1
Electronic 1	.1	3,500¥	5/48 hrs	1
Electronic 2	.1	7,500¥	5/48 hrs	1
Electronic 3	.1	11,000¥	8/48 hrs	1

MATRIXWARE

	Essence Cost	Cost	Availability	Street Index
MPCP	See Text	See Text	12/60 days	4
Persona Module	.3	See Text	Varies/12 days	Varies
Hardening	.3	See Text	Varies/8 days	Varies
Memory/Storage	Mp/300	Mp x 150¥	3/24 hrs	.8
Transfer	.1	See Text	Varies/10 days	Varies
Response	.2	See Text	Varies/14 days	Varies

BODYWARE

	Essence Cost	Cost	Availability	Street Index
Bone Lacing				
Plastic	.5	7,500¥	5/14 days	1.5
Aluminum	1.15	25,000¥	5/14 days	1.5
Titanium	2.25	75,000¥	5/14 days	1.5
Fingertip Compartment	.1	3/24 hrs	3,000¥	1
Hand Razors	.1	3/72 hrs	4,500¥	1
Hydraulic Jack				
(Levels 1–6)	.25	Level x 5,000¥	5/6 days	1
Muscle Replacement				
(Maximum Rating 4)	Rating	Rating x 20,000¥	4/4 days	1
Retractable Razors	.2	9,000¥	5/72 hrs	1
Retractable Spur	.3	11,500¥	5/72 hrs	1
Smartcam Link	.5	2,500¥	4/48 hrs	2
Smartlink (Lvl I)	.5	2,500¥	3/36 hrs	1
Smartlink (Lvl II)	.5	3,200¥	6/48 hrs	2
Spur	.1	7,000¥	3/72 hrs	1
Voice Modulator	.2	45,000¥	2/24 hrs	1
Increased Volume	—	10,000¥	2/24 hrs	1
Tonal Shift	—	25,000¥	2/24 hrs	1
Secondary Pattern (illegal)	—	50,000¥	6/7 days	2
Playback	.2	40,000¥	4/48 hrs	1
Limbs				
Built-In Device	—	4 x Normal Cost	Varies	Varies
Built-In Smartgun Link	.25	2,500¥	6/4 days	1.5
Cyber Guns				
Hold-Out Pistol	—	250¥	8/7 days	2
Light Pistol	—	650¥	8/7 days	2
Machine Pistol	—	900¥	8/7 days	2
Submachine Gun	—	1,800¥	8/7 days	2
Heavy Pistol	—	800¥	8/7 days	2
Shotgun	—	1,200¥	8/7 days	2
Cyber Limb	1	100,000¥	4/4 days	1
Increased Strength	—	Level x 150,000¥	6/4 days	1.5
Simple Replacement	1	50,000¥	4/48 hrs	1
Simrigs				
Baseline Cyberware Simrig	2	300,000¥	8/12 days	3
Full-X Cyberware Simrig	2	500,000¥	6/12 days	3
Baseline Induction Simrig	2	50,000¥	6/4 days	2
Simlinks				
Internal (Rating 1-10)	.6 + (Rating x .05)	70k¥ + (10k¥ x Rating)	8/7 days	3
Boosted Reflexes				
Level 1	.5	15,000¥	3/24 hrs	1
Level 2	1.25	40,000¥	3/24 hrs	1.25
Level 3	2.8	90,000¥	3/24 hrs	1.5
Dermal Plating				
Level 1	.5	6,000¥	4/12 days	1
Level 2	1	15,000¥	4/12 days	1
Level 3	1.5	45,000¥	4/12 days	1
Filtration Systems				
Air	Rating ÷ 10	Rating x 15,000¥	6/4 days	1
Blood	Rating ÷ 5	Rating x 10,000¥	6/4 days	1
Ingested Toxin	Rating ÷ 5	Rating x 10,000¥	6/4 days	1
Skill Hardwires				
Level 1–4	Level x .2	Level x 5,000¥	6/10 days	1
Level 5–8	Level x .25	Level x 50,000¥	12/14 days	1.5
Level 9–10	Level x .3	Level x 500,000¥	12/14 days	1.5

Skillwires	Essence Cost	Cost	Availability	Street Index
Rating 1–3	.1 x Rating	Rating x 10,000¥	4/10 days	1
Rating 4–6	.2 x Rating	Rating x 100,000¥	5/10 days	1
Rating 7–9	.3 x Rating	Rating x 1,000,000¥	12/20 days	1
Skillwire Plus				
Level 1–3	Level x .1	Level x 15,000¥	4/10 days	1
Level 4–6	Level x .2	Level x 125,000¥	5/10 days	1
Level 7–9	Level x .3	Level x 1,000,000 ¥	12/20 days	1
Vehicle Control Rig				
Level 1	2	12,000¥	6/48 hrs	1
Level 2	3	60,000¥	8/48 hrs *OK*	1.25
Level 3	5	300,000¥	8/48 hrs *OK*	1.5
Wired Reflexes				
Level 1	2	55,000¥	4/8 days	1
Level 2	3	165,000¥	4/8 days	1
Level 3	5	500,000¥	8/14 days *OK*	1

Skillsofts	Concealability	Base Price	Availability	Street Index
Knowsoft	24	Mp x 150¥	5/4 days	1.25
Activesoft	24	Mp x 100¥	6/4 days	1.25
Linguasoft	24	Mp x 50¥	6/36 hrs	1.25
Datasoft	24	Mp x 100¥*	4/4 days	1.25

*More valuable data will cost more.

BIOWARE

	Body Index	Base Price	Availability	Street Index
Adrenal Pump				
Level 1	1.25	60,000¥	10/16 days	3
Level 2	2.5	100,000¥	10/16 days	3
Cerebral Booster				
Level 1	.4	50,000¥	6/14 days	2
Level 2	.8	110,000¥	6/14 days	2
Damage Compensator				
Level 1–2	.2/Level	25,000¥/Level	6/6 days	2.5
Level 3–5	.2/Level	50,000¥/Level	10/6 days	2.
Level 6–9	.2/Level	100,000¥/Level	12/6 days	2.5
Enhanced Articulation	.6	40,000¥	5/6 days	1.5
Extended Volume				
Level 1	.2	8,000¥	4/4 days	1
Level 2	.3	15,000¥	4/4 days	1
Level 3	.4	25,000¥	4/4 days	1
Mnemonic Enhancer	.2/Level	15,000¥/Level	6/7 days	1
Muscle Augmentation	.8/Level	45,000¥/Level	6/6 days	.9
Nephritic Screen	.4	20,000¥	4/4 days	1
Orthoskin				
Level 1	.5	25,000¥	8/8 days	.8
Level 2	1	60,000¥	8/8 days	.8
Level 3	1.5	100,000¥	8/8 days	.8
Pain Editor	.6	60,000¥	6/6 days	1.2
Pathogenic Defense	.2/Level	24,000¥/Level	4/4 days	1.5
Platelet Factory	.4	30,000¥	5/8 days	1.5
Reflex Recorder				
Concentration	.1*	10,000¥*	5/6 days	1.5
General	.25*	25,000¥*	8/6 days	1.5
Suprathyroid Gland	1.4	50,000¥	8/12 days	2.5

	Body Index	Base Price	Availability	Street Index
Symbiotes				
Level 1	.4	15,000¥	5/10 days	1
Level 2	.7	35,000¥	5/10 days	1
Level 3	1	60,000¥	5/10 days	1
Synaptic Accelerator				
Level 1	.3	75,000¥	6/12 days	2
Level 2	1.6	200,000¥	6/12 days	2
Synthacardium				
Level 1	.2	6,000¥	4/10 days	1.5
Level 2	.3	15,000¥	4/10 days	1.5
Tailored Pheromones				
Level 1	.4	20,000¥	12/14 days	2
Level 2	.6	45,000¥	12/14 days	2
Toxin Exhaler	.6	30,000¥+	10/4 days	3
Toxin Extractor	.2/Level	24,000¥/Level	4/4 days	1
Tracheal Filter	.2/Level	30,000¥/Level	4/4 days	1
Trauma Damper	.4	40,000¥	6/8 days	2

GENE-TECH

	Base Price	Availability	Street Index
Antibac			
Level 1–3	Level x 500¥	4/48 hrs	1
Level 4–6	Level x 1,000¥	4/48 hrs	1
Level 7–9	Level x 1,500¥	4/48 hrs	1
Level 10+	Level x 2,500¥	4/48 hrs	1
Binder			
Level 1–3	Level x 300¥	4/32 hrs	2
Level 4–6	Level x 600¥	4/32 hrs	2
Level 7–9	Level x 900¥	4/32 hrs	2
Level 10+	Level x 1,500¥	4/32 hrs	2
Doom	500¥/dose	14/30 days	5
Gamma-Anthrax	180¥/dose	14/30 days	6
Gene Therapy			
Cleansing	50,000¥	6/30 days	2.5
Genetic Correction	60,000¥	6/30 days	2.5
Reconstruct/Healing	100,000¥	6/30 days	2.5
Other	50,000¥+	6/30 days	2.5
Immunization			
Single	40,000¥ per treatment	6/20 days	2
Full Spectrum	300,000¥	6/20 days	2
Leónization	2,000,000¥ + 100,000¥	6/30 days	2.5
Myco-Protein	25¥/kg	It's everywhere	1
Zeta-Interpheron			
Level 1–3	Level x 400¥	4/32 hrs	2
Level 4–6	Level x 800¥	4/32 hrs	2
Level 7–9	Level x 1,200¥	4/32 hrs	2
Level 10+	Level x 2,000¥	4/32 hrs	2

COMPOUNDS

ACTH	100¥/6 doses	5/12 hrs	1
Atropine	600¥/dose	5/12 hrs	1
Carcerands	See Text	4/10 days	2
Cyanide	360¥/dose	3/48 hrs	.5
Dikote™	1,000¥/100cm^3	6/14 days	10
DMSO	10¥+	2/12 hrs	1.5
Hyper	180¥/dose	4/24 hrs	.9

	Base Price	Availability	Street Index
Kamikaze	50¥/dose	5/4 days	5
MAO	280¥/dose	5/36 hrs	2
Oxygenated Flourocarbons	750¥ per liter	4/48 hrs	1
Ruthenium Polymers	10,000¥/m^2 +	5/14 days	7.5

CYBERDECKS AND PROGRAMS

CYBERDECKS

	Persona	Hardening	Memory	Storage	Load	I/O
Radio Shack PCD-100	2	0	10	50	5	1
Allegiance Alpha	3	1	10	50	5	1
Sony CTY-360	6	3	50	100	20	10
Fuchi Cyber-4	6	3	100	500	20	20
Fuchi Cyber-6	8	4	100	500	50	30
Fuchi Cyber-7	10	4	200	1,000	50	40
Fairlight Excalibur	12	5	500	1,000	100	50

	Availability	Cost	Street Index
Radio Shack PCD-100	4/7 days	6,800¥	1
Allegiance Alpha	4/7 days	12,600¥	1
Sony CTY-360	4/7 days	99, 400¥	1
Fuchi Cyber-4	4/7 days	121, 400¥	1
Fuchi Cyber-6	6/7 days	334,500¥	1
Fuchi Cyber-7	10/7 days	1,112,100¥	1
Fairlight Excalibur	22/7 days	5,529,600¥	1

Cyberdeck System Additions

	Availability	Cost	Street Index
Hitcher Jack	2/48 hrs	MPCP x 100¥	1
Off-line Storage	2/24 hrs	1¥ x Mp	1
Vidscreen Display	2/24 hrs	100¥	1
Response Increase			
Level 1	6/48 hrs	(MPCP x MPCP) x 100¥	1
Level 2	8/72 hrs	(MPCP x MPCP) x 400¥	2
Level 3	12/7 days	(MPCP x MPCP) x 900¥	2

PROGRAM SIZES

Persona Programs	Size (in Mp)
Bod	(Rating x Rating) x 3
Evasion	(Rating x Rating) x 3
Masking	(Rating x Rating) x 2
Sensors	(Rating x Rating) x 2

Utility Programs	
Analyze	(Rating x Rating) x 3
Armor	(Rating x Rating) x 3
Attack	(Rating x Rating) x 2
Auto Exec	(Rating x Rating)
Blind	(Rating x Rating) x 3
Browse	(Rating x Rating)
Cloak	(Rating x Rating) x 3
Compressor	(Rating x Rating) x 2
Controller	(Rating x Rating) x 4

Utility Programs	Size (in Mp)
Deception	(Rating x Rating) x 2
Decrypt	(Rating x Rating) x 2
Evaluate	(Rating x Rating) x 2
Hog	(Rating x Rating) x 3
Medic	(Rating x Rating) x 4
Mirrors	(Rating x Rating) x 3
Poison	(Rating x Rating) x 3
Relocate	(Rating x Rating) x 2
Restore	(Rating x Rating) x 3
Restrict	(Rating x Rating) x 3
Reveal	(Rating x Rating) x3
Scanner	(Rating x Rating) x3
Shield	(Rating x Rating) x 4
Sift	(Rating x Rating)
Sleaze	(Rating x Rating) x 3
Slow	(Rating x Rating) x 4
Smoke	(Rating x Rating) x 2

PROGRAM COSTS AND AVAILABILITY

Persona Programs

Rating	Availability	Cost	Street Index
1–3	3/7 days	Size x 100¥	1
4–6	6/7 days	Size x 500¥	1.5
7–9	12/14 days	Size x 1,000¥	2
10+	24/30 days	Size x 5,000¥	3

Utility Programs

Rating	Availability	Cost	Street Index
1–3	2/7 days	Size x 100¥	1
4–6	4/7 days	Size x 200¥	1.5
7–9	8/14 days	Size x 500¥	2
10+	16/100 days	Size x 1,000¥	3

BIOTECH

	Rating	Availability	Weight	Cost	Street Index
Medkit	3	2/24 hrs	3	200¥	1.5
Medkit Supplies	—	2/24 hrs	—	50¥	1.5
Stabilization Unit	2	12/1 mth	30	10,000¥	3
Deluxe Unit	6	16/1 mth	35	20,000¥	3
DocWagon™ Contract					
Basic Service	—	On payment	—	5,000¥ per year	—
Gold Service	—	On payment	—	25,000¥ per year	—
Platinum Service	—	On payment	—	50,000¥ per year	—
Super-Platinum Service	—	On payment	—	100,000¥ per year	—
Slap Patches					
Antidote Patch	Maximum 8	6/72 hrs	—	Rating x 50¥	2
Stimulant Patch	Maximum 6	2/24 hrs	—	Rating x 25¥	1
Tranq Patch	Maximum 10	4/48 hrs	—	Rating x 20¥	2
Trauma Patch	—	4/48 hrs	—	500¥	4

MAGICAL EQUIPMENT

FOCI

	Availability	Cost	Street Index
Specific Spell Focus	4/48 hrs	Rating x 45,000¥	2
Spell Type Focus	5/48 hrs	Rating x 75,000¥	2
Spirit Focus	4/48 hrs	Rating x 60,000¥	2
Power Focus	6/72 hrs	Rating x 105,000¥	2
Spell Lock	2/48 hrs	45,000¥	2
Weapon Foci	8/72 hrs	[(Reach +1) x 100,000¥] + Rating x 90,000¥	3

MAGICAL SUPPLIES

	Availability	Cost	Street Index
Elemental Conjuration Materials	(Force)/24 hrs	Force x 1,000¥	1
Medicine Lodge Materials	(Rating)/24 hrs	Rating x 500¥	1
Fetish Focus	3/26 hrs	Rating x 3,000¥	1
Ally Conjuring Material	(Force)/36 hrs	1,000 per unit	1
Ward Casting Materials	(Force)/36 hrs	1,000 per unit	1
Watcher Casting Materials	(Force)/36 hrs	1,000 per unit	1
Expendable Fetishes			
Combat	2/24 hrs	20¥	1
Detection	2/24 hrs	5¥	1
Healing	2/24 hrs	50¥	1
Illusion	2/24 hrs	10¥	1
Manipulation	2/24 hrs	30¥	1
Hermetic Library (any magic skill)			
Computer Media (disk)	(Rating)/7 days	(Rating x Rating) x 1,000¥	2
Chip	(Rating)/7 days	(Rating x Rating) x 1,200¥	2
Hardcopy	(Rating)/14 days	(Rating x Rating) x 2,000¥	3
Reusable Fetishes			
Combat	3/24 hrs	200¥	1
Detection	3/24 hrs	50¥	1
Healing	3/24 hrs	500¥	1
Illusion	3/24 hrs	100¥	1
Manipulation	3/24 hrs	300¥	1

Ritual Sorcery Materials

Detection	3/24 hrs	100¥ x spell Force	1
Healing	3/24 hrs	500¥ x spell Force	1
Illusion	3/24 hrs	100¥ x spell Force	1
Manipulation	3/24 hrs	1,000¥ x spell Force	1

Enchanting Material Costs

Material	Raw Form	Refined Form	Radical Form
Herbals	50	100	200
Crystals	100	200	400
Semi-precious Gems	200	400	800
Precious Gems	500	1,000	2,000
Iron	50	100	200
Copper	100	200	400
Silver	300	600	1,200
Gold	10,000	20,000	40,000
Mercury	600	1,200	2,400
Tin	30	60	120
Lead	30	60	120

Orichalum: 88,000 per unit

Spell Formulas

Drain Level	Price	Drain Level	Prive
L	50 x Force	M	100 x Force
S	500 x Force	D	1,000 x Force

VEHICLES

Note: Vehicles generally have an Availability equal to Cost/10,000. The base time is equal to 1/2 the Availability (round down) in days. Street Index is .75 for vehicles that cost less than 10,000¥, 1 for up to 50,000¥, and 2 for more than 50,000¥.

	Handling	Speed	Body	Armor	Signature	APilot	Cost
GROUND							
Cars							
Chrysler-Nissan Jackrabbit (Elec.)	3/8	25/75	1	0	5	1	15,000¥
(MultiFuel)	3/8	30/90	1	0	3	1	18,000¥
Eurocar Westwind 2000	3/8	70/210	2	0	2	3	100,000¥
Ford Americar	4/8	35/105	2	0	2	2	20,000¥
Honda-GM 3220 ZX	4/8	40/120	2	0	2	1	30,000¥
Honda-GM 3220 ZX Turbo	4/8	50/150	2	0	1	2	45,000¥
Leyland-Zil Tsarina (Elec.)	4/8	25/75	1	0	5	1	10,000¥
(MultiFuel)	4/8	30/90	1	0	2	1	12,000¥
Mitsubishi Nightsky	4/8	45/120	5	3	4	4	250,000¥
Mitsubishi Runabout	4/8	25/75	1	0	5	1	10,000¥
Rolls-Royce Phaeton	4/4	60/180	5	6	2	4	500,000¥
Saab Dynamit 778TI	4/8	80/250	2	3	1	3	250,000¥
Toyota Elite	4/8	40/120	4	0	2	4	125,000¥
Volkswagon Electro	3/6	20/60	1	0	5	0	8,000¥
Bikes							
BMW Blitzen 2050	3/4	95/285	3	6	1	2	25,000¥
Dodge Scoot	3/6	20/60	1	0	4	0	2,000¥
Entertainment Systems Papoose	3/6	30/90	1	0	5	0	6,000¥
Harley-Davidson Scorpion	4/5	50/150	3	3	2	2	15,000¥
Honda Viking	3/5	50/150	4	3	1	2	17,000¥
Hyundai Offroader	4/2	60/180	2	0	2	1	12,500¥
Gaz-Niki White Eagle	3/3	60/180	3	0	1	0	15,000¥
Suzuki Aurora	2/4	70/210	1	0	1	1	15,000¥
Thundercload Pinto	4/2	20/60	3	0	2	0	35,000¥
Yamaha Rapier	3/6	65/195	1	0	1	1	10,000¥

	Handling	Speed	Body	Armor	Signature	APilot	Cost
Trucks							
Ares Roadmaster	4/10	30/90	4	0	2	2	45,000¥
Conestoga Trailblazer	4/8	30/90	5	0	2	2	150,000¥
Ford-Canada Bison	4/3	45/135	5	6	4	3	150,000¥
Gaz-Willy Nomad	3/3	30/90	3	0	2	2	50,000¥
GMC 4201	3/6	35/85	5	3	2	2	75,000¥
GMC Bulldog Step-Van (MultiFuel)	4/8	35/85	4	3	2	2	35,000¥
GMC Bulldog Step-Van (Courier)	4/6	35/85	4	6	1	2	60,000¥
Landrover Model 2046 (short)	3/3	30/90	2	0	2	1	35,000¥
Landrover Model 2046 (long)	3/3	30/90	3	0	2	2	45,000¥
Leyland-Rover Transport (basic-Elec.)	4/8	25/75	3	0	5	2	25,000¥
(basic- MultiFuel)	4/8	35/105	3	0	2	2	30,000¥
Nissan-Holden Brumbry	4/3	30/90	2	0	2	2	25,000¥
Nordkapp-Conestoga Bergan (Command)	3/6	30/90	6	6	2	4	600,000¥
(Cargo)	3/6	30/90	5	3	2	—	200,000¥
Renault-Fiat Eurovan	4/10	35/105	3	0	2	1	25,000¥
Rolls-Royce Prairie Cat	2/3	40/120	3	3	2	3	275,000¥
ToyotaCorp Gopher	4/4	35/105	2	0	2	2	25,000¥
Volkswagon SuperKombi III	4/8	35/105	4	3	2	3	Varies
HOVERCRAFT							
Chrysler-Nissan G12a	4	40/120	4	0	5	2	50,000¥
GMC-Beachcraft Vacationer	4	35/120	4	0	3	3	100,000¥
GMC-Nissan Hovertruck	4	40/120	4	0	5	1	100,000¥
Mostrans KVP-14T	4	60/180	4	0	3	1	250,000¥
BOATS							
Water Jet Bike							
Suzuki Watersport (Standard)	2	15/45	1	0	3	0	1,2000¥
Suzuki Watersport (Electric)	2	10/30	1	0	5	0	1,300¥
Motorboats							
Aztech Nightrunner	3	25/75	2	0	4	3	30,000¥
Electric		10/30			8		
Colorado Craft Cigarette	4/5	25/75	2	0	3	2	35,000¥
Marine Technologies Dolphin II	3	15/45	3	0	3	2	50,000¥
Harland & Wolff Classique	5	15/45	6	0	2	4	3,500,000¥
Samuvani Criscraft Otter	4	15/45	2	0	3	2	20,000¥
Zemlya-Poltava Swordsman	4	25/75	3	0	3	2	30,000¥
Sailboats							
Sendanko Marlin	2	20/30	2	0	5	0	15,000¥
AIRCRAFT							
Winged Planes							
Cessna C750	5	340/680	3	0	2	2	200,000¥
Embraer-Dassault Mistral	4	300/450	4	0	3	2	375,000¥
Fiat-Fokker Cloud Nine	4	300/450	3	0	3	2	175,000¥
Hawker-Ridley HS-895 Skytruck	5	400/600	5	0	3	2	2,500,000¥
Lear-Cessna Platinum I	4	400/550	5	0	3	3	500,000¥
Lear-Cessna Platinum II	5	800/1600	5	3	3	4	1,500,000¥
Rotor Craft							
Agusta-Cierva Plutocrat	4	200/450	4	3	4	4	950,000¥
Ares Dragon	5/7	140/320	6	0	3	3	600,000¥
Federated Boeing Commuter	5	140/320	3	0	3	3	625,000¥
Hughes Aerospace Airstar 2050	4	190/260	4	6	3	4	900,000¥
Hughes WK-2 Stallion	5	170/250	4	0	4	3	300,000¥

TABLES

	Handling	Speed	Body	Armor	Signature	APilot	Cost
Lighter-Than-Air Craft							
Airship Industries Skyswimmer	3	90/180	6	3	8	2	100,000¥
Goodyear Commuter-47	3	150/300	8	3	8	2	225,000¥
Luftschiffbau Zeppelin LZ-2049	3	100/250	12	6	8	2	750,000¥
ORBITALS AND SEMI-BALLISTICS							
Arrow HSCT	5	1,500/2,900	4	3	2	4	10 M¥
China Clipper Suborbital	5	10k/24k	5	6	1	3	100 M¥
General Dynamics SV250 Semiballistic	6	10k/29k	5	6	1	4	750 M¥
MILITARY, SECURITY AND RESTRICTED ISSUE							
Aircraft/Rotorcraft							
Aztechnology Aguilar-EX	4	280/560	3	6	4 (8)	4	2,600,000¥
BAC-Dassault-MBB EFA variants	3	950/1,900	4	6	4	3	5,000,000¥
CASA J-239 Raven	3	200/400	3	0	4	1	175,000¥
Doc Wagon™ CRT Air Unit	5	140/320	3	0	3	3	N/A
Doc Wagon™ Osprey II	5	190/380	3	3	2	3	N/A
Doc Wagon™ SRT Helicopter	5	170/250	4	0	4	3	N/A
Doc Wagon™ WK-2 Stallion Variant	5	165/235	5	6	4	3	N/A
Lockheed C-260 Transport	7	150/350	5	12	4	3	700,000¥
Moonlight Aerospace Avenger	4	100/200	3	9	8	2	250,000¥
Nightglider	3	15/60	1	0	12	1	45,000¥
Northrup PRC-42B Wasp	3	65/130	1	0	3	0	220,000¥
PRC-42F	2	65/130	2	6	5	0	294,000¥
Northrup PRC-44B Yellowjacket	4	65/130	2	0	3	0	280,000¥
PRC-44F	3	65/130	3	9	5	0	390,000¥
Armored Vehicles							
Ferrari Appaloosa Light Scout	2/3	100/200	3	9	5	2	1,000,000¥
LAV-93 Devil Rat APC	5/3	25/75	3	12	6	2	250,000¥
LAV-103 Striker Light Tank	6/4	25/75	5	15	6	2	480,000¥
Thunderbirds							
GMC Banshee	3	650/1,000	6	18	5	2	10M¥+
Ground/ACV Vehicles							
Ares Citymaster	4/10	30/120	4	12	2	3	500,000¥
Ares Mobmaster	4/10	30/120	5	15	2	5	3,650,000¥
Doc Wagon™ Citymaster Varient	4/10	35/140	4	6	2	3	N/A
Doc Wagon™ CRT Ambulance	4/10	30/75	5	0	2	2	N/A
Doc Wagon™ SRT Ambulance	4/10	30/75	4	0	4	3	N/A
Chrysler Nissan Patrol	4/8	60/180	3	6	4	3	100,000¥
General Products Cop	4/9	30/90	1	3	4	1	25,000¥
GMC Beachcraft Patroller	4	55/165	4	6	5	2	750,000¥
GMC MPUV	5/3	40/120	2	9	4	0	22,000¥
Harley Electroglide-1000	3/4	95/285	3	6	2	1	75,000¥
Sikorsky-Bell Red Ranger	4/6	150/450	2	6	3	3	250,000¥
Water Vehicles							
Blohm & Voss River Commander	4	25/75	6	9 (12)	3	3	300,000¥
GMC Riverine	3	30/90	4	6	3	2	125,000¥
Surfstar Marine Seacop	3	30/90	3	6	3	2	50,000¥
Vectored Thrust							
Federated Boeing Eagle	3	900/1,800	5	12	5	3	50M¥
REMOTES AND DRONES							
Airborne							
Aerodesign Systems Condor LDSD-23	5	20/60	1	0	10	1	2,500¥
Aerodesign Systems Condor II LDSD-41	5	30/90	1	3	11	3	45,000¥
CAS Windjina RPV	3/5	250/500	5	6	4/8	4	75,000¥
GM-Nissan Spotter	3	35/100	2	0	3	2	12,500¥
MCT-Nissan Rotordrone	4	35/70	2	0	3	2	7,500¥

Ground

	Handling	Speed	Body	Armor	Signature	APilot	Cost
Aztech GCR-23C Crawler	4/4	5/15	1	0	4	1	1,250¥
Cyberspace Designs Dalmation	3	35/105	2	0	4	2	15,000¥
Ferret RPD-VI Perimeter Drone	3/5	10/30	1	3	8	3	154,800¥
Gaz-Niki GNRD-71 BIS Snooper	4/3	25/75	1	0	5	1	1,750¥
GM-Nissan Doberman	3/5	35/70	3	6	3	2	10,000¥
Sikorsky-Bell Microskimmer	5	30/90	1	0	3	1	2,750¥
Steel Lynx Ground Combat Drone	4/6	40/80	4	12	5	2	15,000¥

VEHICLE WEAPONS

Note that Availability and Street Index for vehicle-grade weapons are at the gamemaster's discretion.

	Type	Ammo	Mode	Damage	Weight	Cost
Ares Firelance Vehicle Laser	"Assault"	40	SA	15S	48	300,000¥
Generic Autocannon	Cannon	10 (c)	SA	12D	45	12,0000¥
Generic Rocket Launcher	Rocket	6 (b)	SS	as rocket	15	15,000¥
Water Cannon	"Shotgun"	"20"	"SA"	6M Stun	12	20,000¥
Vanquisher Minigun	HMG	Belt (100)	FA	10S	45	75,000¥
Vengeance Minigun	MMG	Belt (100)	FA	9S	30	50,000¥
Victory Rotary Assault Cannon	Cannon	Belt (50)	FA	18D	90	90,000¥
Vigilant Rotary Autocannon	Cannon	Belt (25)	FA	20D	60	125,000¥

	Intelligence	Damage	Cost
Saab-Saaker AAM (Basic)	6	18D	25,000¥
(Improved)	7	18D	50,000¥
Hyndai Advanced AAM (Basic)	8	18D	100,000¥
(Improved)	9	18D	150,000¥
Ares Dragon AAM (Dogfight)	8	20D	500,000¥
(Attack)	9	20D	1,500,000¥
Mitusbishi-GM Bandit AGM			
(Bandit)	6	varies	10,000¥
(Super Bandit)	6	varies	15,000¥
General Products Rockets			
(7.62 cm)	N/A	3D/rocket	1,000¥
(12.7 cm)	N/A	7D/rocket	1,500¥

RIGGER AND VEHICLE GEAR

	Availability	Cost	Street Index
Remote Control Gear	4/72 hrs	2,500¥ x Body	2
Vehicle Control Gear	4/7 days	2,800¥	2

	Rating	Weight	Cost	Availability	Street Index
Remote Control Deck	Slave Ports	2 x Rating	5,000¥ x Rating	4/72 hrs	2

VEHICLE SMOKE GENERATOR

	Number of Charges	Cost
Small Smoke Generator	6	700¥
Large Smoke Generator	12	1,000¥

Each charge covers a given area. For smoke rules, see p. 85.

ABLATIVE VEHICLE ARMOR

Armor Level	Availability	Cost	Street Index
1	8/14 days	700¥	2
2	12/14 days	1,600¥	2
3	14/21 days	2,500¥	2

>>>>(Slot & run, chummer.)<<<<

You're busy. Staying alive in the sprawl is a full-time job, so we'll make it quick. You need to jack into the Shadowrun Network©, the only org licensed by FASA to give you what you need: the latest news, info and rumors from the streets of 2053.

>>>>(What's my cut?)<<<<

You want a pretty certificate? Go join a corp. We're not some drekky little fan club. We're a network, with an accent on the work. For your donation of $20.00 (S&H can be extra), you get four issues of our quarterly newsmagazine, **KA•GE**™. **KA•GE**™ is 48 pages of chiptruth that covers the streets from every angle, whether you want magic, matrix, or Mossberg. We give you fiction, new gear, spells, contacts and archetypes, all wrapped around a tough scenario. You'll also get the hottest paydata on FASA's new products, long before they hit the streets.

>>>>(Cut to the chase.)<<<<

For your sixteen bucks you get:
- Four 48 page issues of Ka•ge with:
  - Access to restricted FASA information
  - Stats on more & better tools of the trade
  - New contacts
  - New archetypes
  - New locations w/ Maps
  - Product Reviews
  - New Scenarios
  - Convention Information
  - New Fiction
  - The chance to have your own artwork and prose published!

(Please use a pen and print clearly)
Name: _____
Street Address: _____
City: _____ State: _____ Zip: _____
Phone: _____

This is a...(Check one)

☐ New Membership   ☐ Renewal

...If Renewal, list Membership # _____

☐ Full Membership $20.00

In order for Ka•ge to reach me I'll need...

☐ US 1st Class postage _ _ _ _ _ _ _ _ _ _ _ _ _ _ _ Included
☐ Canada/Mexico 1st Class postage _ _ _ _ _ _ _ _ _ $4.00
☐ Overseas 1st Class postage _ _ _ _ _ _ _ _ _ _ _ _ $6.00
Total amount included _ _ _ _ _ _ _ _ _ _ _ _ | $ |

Make all Checks/Money Orders payable to

SHADOWRUN NETWORK©
AND IN UNITED STATES DOLLARS ONLY

Mail to:
AWOL Productions
2101 West Broadway #305
PO Box 6018
Columbia, MO 65205-6018

• **FIN** •